CANADA
Its Land and People

A Reidmore Book

CAN

Its Land a

ADA

d People

by Dr. Donald Massey
with Dr. Bryan Connors

A Reidmore Book

Canadian Cataloguing in Publication Data

Massey, Donald L., 1936-
Canada, its land & people

Includes index.

ISBN 0--919091-20-2

1. Canada - Description and travel - 1981-
Juvenile literature. I. Title.
FC58.M37 1985   j917.1   C85-091578-3
F1008.2.M37 1985

Original illustrations, charts & diagrams:
  Gundra Kucy
Original maps:
  Don Taschuk, with Dr. Lillian Wonders
Typesetting & Production:
  Pièce de Résistance Ltd., Edmonton
Colour Separations & Stripping:
  Color Graphics Alberta Ltd., Edmonton
Printing:
  Kromar Printing Ltd., Winnipeg

A Reidmore Book
Edmonton, Alberta, Canada

Second printing,
February, 1987

Acknowledgements
The publishers wish to gratefully acknowledge the financial support of the Alberta Literary Arts Foundation, Alberta Culture, Nova-Chem Laboratories Inc. and Dr. Erick Schmidt.

Contents

Unit 1

Your Country

The best way to learn about your country would be to travel from place to place and visit with the people who live there. For most of us that is impossible. We have to learn about Canada in other ways. This book will help us do that. Through the use of maps, case studies, charts, graphs, sketches, photographs, and drawings, we will begin to learn about Canada.

To help you organize information about your country, symbols have been used. Each one tells you what you will be learning in that section of the book.

The Landscape

Each time you see this symbol you will learn something about the place. What is the land like? What kind of weather and climate is found here? What resources are used by the people in the area?

FIGURE 1

FIGURE 2

Make a sketch of each kind of land shown in the figures.

FIGURE 3

FIGURE 4

The People

Each time you see this symbol you will learn about people who live in the place. Who are they? How do they earn a living? What are their hopes and fears?

FIGURE 5

FIGURE 6

List the jobs being done by these Canadians.

FIGURE 7

FIGURE 8

2

FIGURE 9

FIGURE 10

Name the kind of transportation shown in each figure.

FIGURE 11

FIGURE 12

Links

Each time you see this symbol you will learn about how places and communities are linked together. You will also learn how communities are linked with each other.

FIGURE 13

How are these central places the same? different?

FIGURE 14

Central Places

Each time you see this symbol you will
learn about central places. From shopping
centres to villages and large cities, people have
organized places where they live, meet, do
business, and carry on other activities. These
places are known as central places.

4

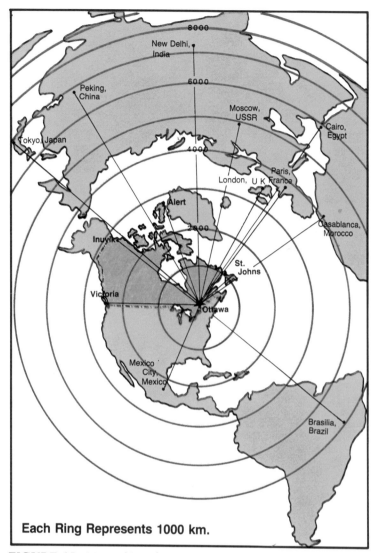

Each Ring Represents 1000 km.

FIGURE 15: Map of North America.

Where is Canada located?

Canada is a vast and empty land. In size, our country is the second largest in the world. Only the **Soviet Union** is larger. Our country takes up most of the northern part of **North America**. Three oceans — the **Pacific**, the **Arctic**, and the **Atlantic** — touch our shores. We share a long border with the **United States of America**. Part of that border crosses the **Great Lakes**. These lakes are the largest fresh water lakes in the world. We have a huge gulf or inland sea called **Hudson Bay**.

Read The Map

1. How many kilometres from Ottawa is **Alert? Victoria? St. John's? Inuvik?**
2. About how far is it from Canada's Pacific to its Atlantic shore?
3. Who are Canada's neighbours to the north?

5

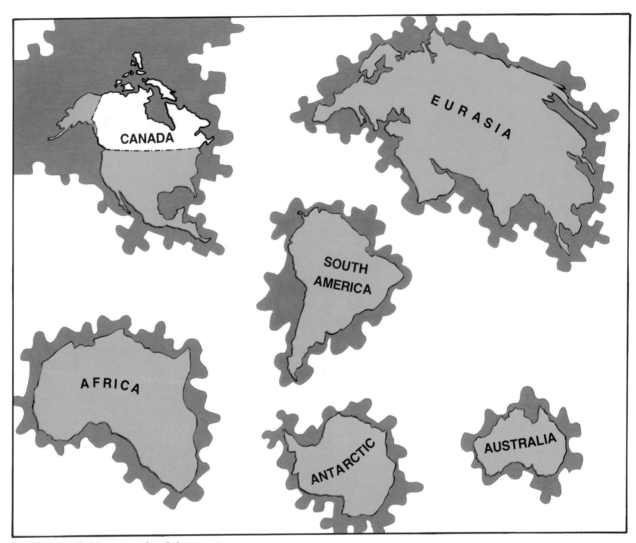

FIGURE 16: Name each of the continents.

Canada's Address

Finding places in your community is easy because each building has an address. Finding places on the globe could be very difficult, so geographers have worked out an address system.

This system is made up of two sets of lines. Like streets and avenues they allow us to locate places on the globe.

The equator divides the earth into two equal parts. A set of 90 lines are drawn north

of the equator, and a set of 90 lines are drawn south of the equator. The distance between each line is called a degree. It is shown by the symbol °. The equator then is 0° and the North Pole is 90° North. Most maps do not include all 90 lines. Often only every 10th or 20th are shown. These lines are called the lines of **latitude.**

A second set of lines have been drawn from the North Pole to the South Pole. There are 360 of these lines. Line 0 goes through

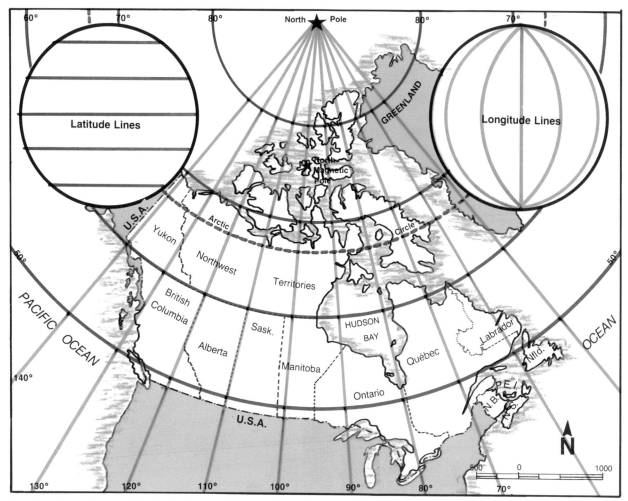

FIGURE 17: Lines of latitude, lines of longitude and important grid lines.

the **observatory** at the town of **Greenwich** in **England**. Lines are numbered East to 180 and West to 180 from Greenwich. The distance between each line is called a degree. These lines are called lines of **longitude**.

Every place on earth then has an address. It is made up of two numbers — the latitude tells how many degrees north or south of the equator the place is located, the longitude tells how many degrees east or west of Greenwich the place is located.

Read the Map

1. Which line of longitude passes along the **Alaska-Yukon border**?
2. What is the latitude line at 60° North called?
3. What latitude line passes along the Canada-United States border?
4. Between which two longitude lines is Canada located?

7

Studying Canada

Canada can be divided into smaller parts for study. By looking at these parts we better understand how we are the same and how we are different across our land.

Geographers have named these parts that they study **regions**. There are many regions we might study. The wheat growing region, the forestry region, or the fishing region are some examples. However, there are seven regions which most Canadians know about. Each unit in this book looks at one of these regions. They are:

The **Cordillera**, Unit 2

The **Plains**, Unit 3

The **North**, Unit 4

The **Canadian Shield**, Unit 5

The **Great Lakes**, Unit 6

The **St. Lawrence River**, Unit 7, and

The **Atlantic**, Unit 8

These regions are shown on the map in Figure 18.

Read the Map

1. List the provinces and territories which are part of each region.
2. List the provinces which are in more than one region.

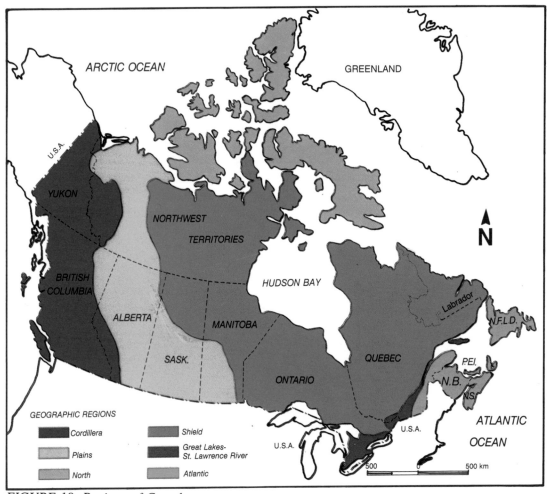

FIGURE 18: Regions of Canada.

8

The Landscape

The landscape of Canada is centred on the region known as the Canadian Shield. This region is partly surrounded by lowlands. Behind the lowlands on three sides are mountain ranges.

The climate of our country is changed by large bodies of water. The Atlantic Ocean, the Pacific Ocean, the Arctic Ocean, Hudson Bay, and the Great Lakes help make winters warmer and summers cooler. As you

FIGURE 20: How are spruce trees and poplar trees different?

FIGURE 19

move inland from these bodies of water the temperatures get colder. The Rocky Mountains, too, change the climate. They stop warm air from the Pacific from reaching the plains and allow cold air from the north to sweep in.

A line known as the **tree-line** crosses Canada. North of this line is the tundra. Only small shrubs and low plants grow here. Trees grow south of this line. The kinds of trees which grow in our forests are shown in Figures 19 and 20.

9

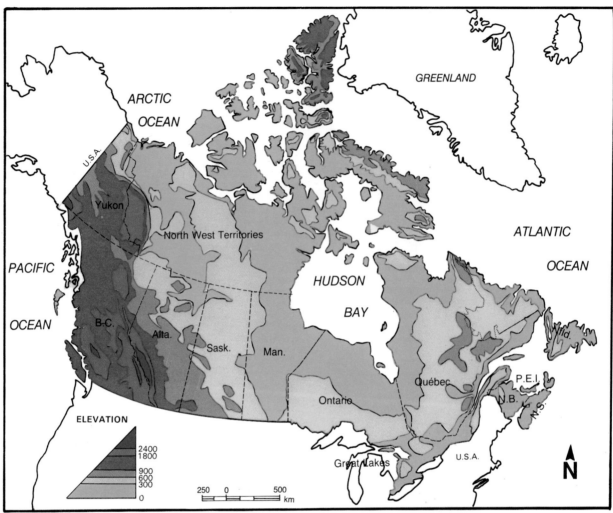

FIGURE 21: Relief map of Canada.

Read the Map

1. What is the subject of Figure 21?
2. What provinces and territories border Hudson Bay?
3. Which provinces have the highest mountains?
4. Which provinces have the lowest elevations?
5. What province borders the Great Lakes?

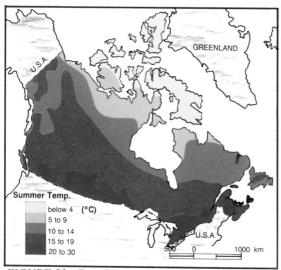

FIGURE 22: *Canadian summer temperatures.*

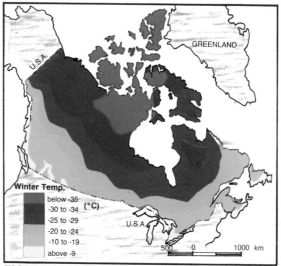

FIGURE 23: *Canadian winter temperatures.*

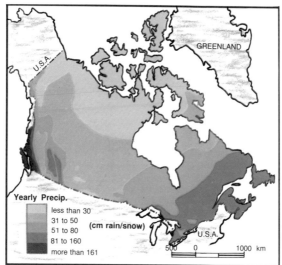

FIGURE 24: *Canadian yearly precipitations.*

Read the Maps

Figures 22, 23 & 24

1. What are the subjects of Figures 22, 23, and 24?

2. Which part of Canada is the driest?

3. Where are the wettest parts of the country located?

4. For which two periods of the year is information about the weather given?

5. Which part of the country has the warmest temperatures in winter?

6. Write a sentence which tells what happens to the temperature as you travel north.

7. Which parts of the country have the warmest temperatures in summer?

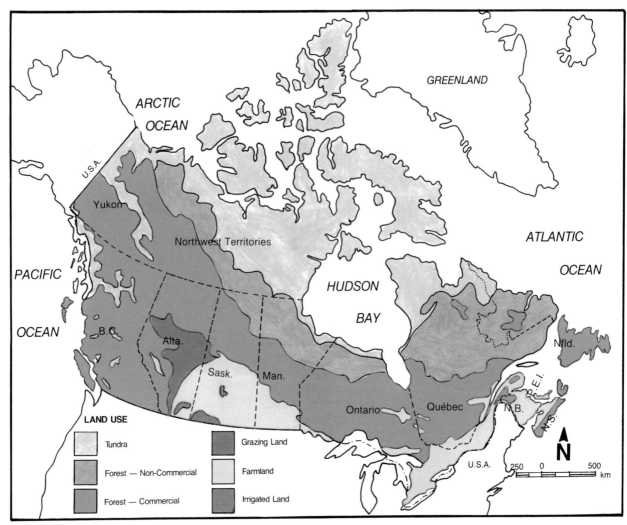

FIGURE 25: Canadian Environments.

Read The Map

Figure 25

1. What is the subject of Figure 25?
2. What covers most of the land in Canada?
3. In which provinces is irrigated land found?
4. Where is most of the farmland in Canada located?

People from Everywhere

Canadians look different from each other. Some have blond hair. Others have black hair. Some are short and others are tall. Some have dark skin and others have light.

Part of the reason for these differences is that people have come from many parts of the world. They have come to make Canada their home. We speak many different languages. To get an idea of the different people in Canada, think of a group of 100 people. They stand for all the people in the country. Figure 30 on the next page show some of the languages spoken.

FIGURE 26

FIGURE 27

When did your family first come to Canada?

FIGURE 28

FIGURE 29

13

MOTHER TONGUE OF 100 CANADIANS

OTHERS 3.6
NATIVE INDIAN
AND INUIT 0.6
POLISH 0.4
CHINESE 0.6
PORTUGUESE 0.6
UKRAINIAN 1.3
GERMAN 2.1
ITALIAN 2.1
FRENCH 26.1
ENGLISH 62.6

FIGURE 30: Is the language your family speaks shown in the chart?

As you can see, most of these languages come from **Europe**. Most Canadians are descended from Europeans. Their grandparents, or other family members came from Europe.

Living Together

Families have rules they follow so that they may live together. When snacks may be eaten, how much television may be watched, when homework must be done, which household jobs each must do, and other rules, help make things fair.

So that we may live together, Canadians have made rules called **laws**. There are laws to help keep us safe and healthy. These laws are made by groups of people called **government**.

It is impossible for everyone in our community, province, or country to meet together to make the laws we need. So, we pick some people to meet and make our laws for us. The day that this is done is called election day. On election day each adult **votes for** (picks) the person they want to be part of the government. We have several governments in Canada.

Your community government is called a **local government**. The leader is usually your **mayor**. The local government makes laws about topics such as the fire department, the police department, and how water will be supplied to the community.

FIGURE 31: A city hall.

Your community is part of a larger area called a **province** or **territory**. The leader of the provincial government is called the **premier**. This government meets in the **capital city** of your province to make laws. What roads will be built, how schools will be paid for, and how hospitals will be run are some of the things they consider.

The provinces and territories make up our country — Canada. The government for Canada is called the **federal government**. The **prime minister** is the leader of this government. How should our country be protected? What mail service does the country need? What radio and television stations should there be in the country? The federal government makes laws about topics such as these.

FIGURE 32: Parliament building, Ottawa.

Using The Information

1. Survey your classmates. Make a pictograph showing the number of students who speak each language in your class.
2. Make a list of the last names of children in your school. Try to determine the mother country of each name.
3. Make a list of the rules you must obey in your community. Give a reason why each rule is needed.
4. Find out the name of:
   a) your mayor
   b) your premier
   c) your prime minister

Many Links

Canadians are joined together in many ways, Trains, trucks, cars, and aircraft move people and goods from community to community. Television and radio make it possible for us to share news from different parts of our country.

Newspapers, magazines, and books help us share and learn about ideas and inventions that Canadians elsewhere are thinking about. Our money, stamps, flag, national anthem and ceremonies help remind us we all belong to a country called Canada.

FIGURE 33: What things make you think about Canada?

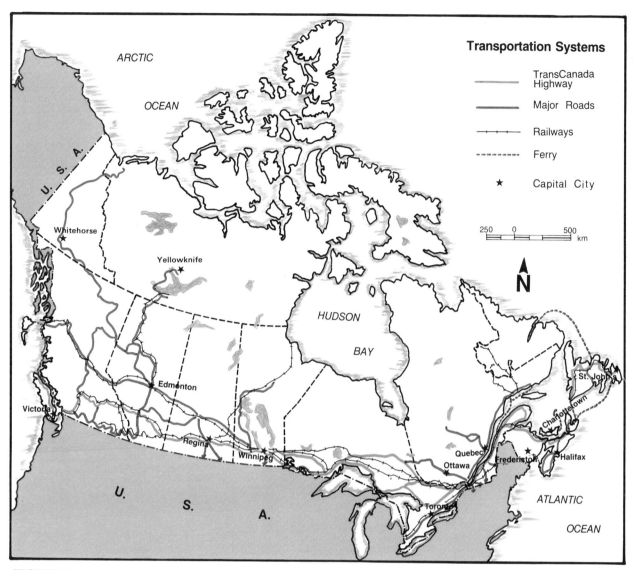

FIGURE 34: *Transportation map of Canada.*

Transportation has always been an important link. Rivers and lakes were the first travelways. From the earliest days railways were used to tie communities together. The railways carried goods and people from one community to another. They were used to bring settlers to various parts of the country. As they carry their loads across the land they help Canadians think about Canada as a country.

Read the Map

1. What is the title of the map?
2. What kinds of transportation links are shown on the map?
3. Sketch the symbols used to show each kind of transportation.
4. Why are most transportation routes near Canada's southern border?

Where We Live

During the past 150 years there has been a change in where Canadians live. Many used to live on farms and in small villages. Now most Canadians live in or near large towns and cities.

This movement to the cities was made possible once farmers produced more than they needed for their own family. This allowed some people to live in the city and buy the food they needed.

Cities cover only a very small part of the land in Canada. However, they are joined by roads, railways, and air routes. There is a great deal of activity in a city. The heat, light, and pollution can be measured from satellites.

The map in Figure 35 shows the provinces and territories of Canada. Figure 36 shows that most Canadians live in towns and cities.

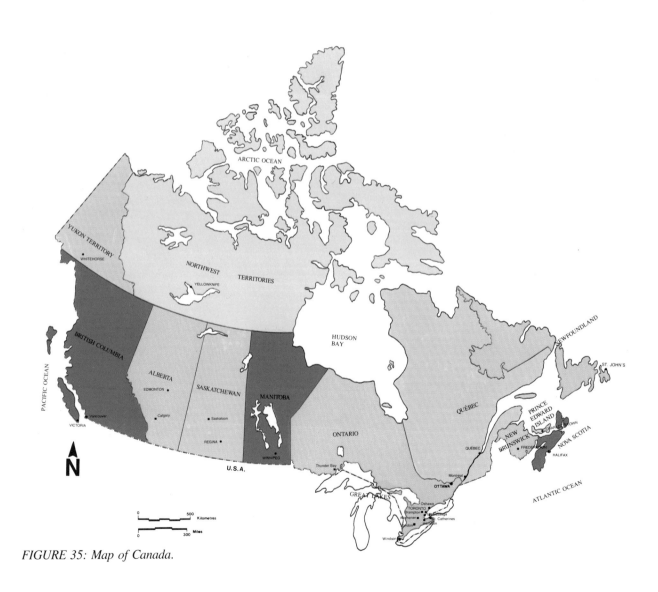

FIGURE 35: Map of Canada.

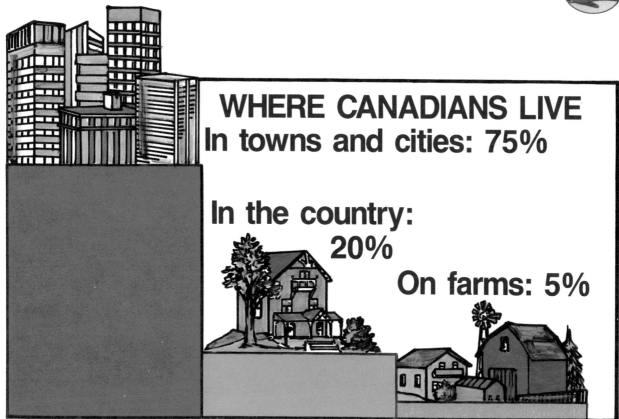

WHERE CANADIANS LIVE
In towns and cities: 75%

In the country:
20%

On farms: 5%

FIGURE 36: Why do most Canadians live in cities?

Read the Map

1. List the names of the provinces and territories.
2. Copy the symbol for capital cities into your notebook.
3. List the capital city of each province and territory.
4. Make a statement which tells about the information shown on Figure 35 and the information given on the graph in Figure 36.
5. The map of Canada may soon change. Find out what those changes might be.

A Vast Land

As you can see from this look at your country, it is large. Trying to understand it will be a lifelong task. In the next units you will explore the regions of Canada and meet some of the Canadians who live there.

FIGURE 1: What is the land like in the·mountains?

Unit 2

Among Mountains and Valleys

What is the cordillera?

Along the western side of North America is a region called the **cordillera.** Cordillera is a Spanish word meaning parallel ridges or mountain ranges. In Canada most of the province of **British Columbia** and the **Yukon Territory** are located in this region.

Sharon Talbot of **Vancouver**, British Columbia, has travelled with her father, who is a sports equipment salesman, to many places on the cordillera. Her scrapbook pictures and maps give an idea of what the region is like.

High mountains, deep valleys, plateaus, and coastal islands make up the land found here. However, what might seem at first to be a jumble of mountains, rivers, lakes, and islands, is not.

FIGURE 2: Cordillera landscape.

FIGURE 3

FIGURE 4

Snapshots from Sharon's scrapbook.

FIGURE 5

FIGURE 6

Read the Pictures

1. In a column, make a list of all the things you see in Sharon's snapshots. Give each item a number.
2. Do any of the items on your list seem to belong together? Write the numbers of these items.
3. Give each group of items you have made a name.
4. Write a sentence about each of the groups you have made.

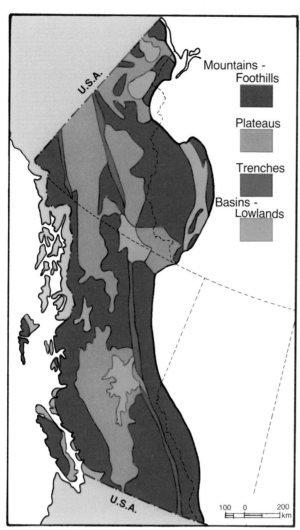

Mountains -
Foothills

Plateaus

Trenches

Basins -
Lowlands

FIGURE 7: Physical features of the cordillera.

Read the Map

1. Make a list of each of the kinds of land shown on the map.
2. Find a photograph in this chapter which shows each landform on your list. Write the number of the photograph beside the landform.

Read the Diagram

1. Near what places on the cordillera was this cross section taken?
2. How does the cross section help show that the word cordillera is a good word to describe the region?
3. List what you would see as you travel west to east across the cordillera.
4. What problems might people living on the cordillera have because of the landscape?

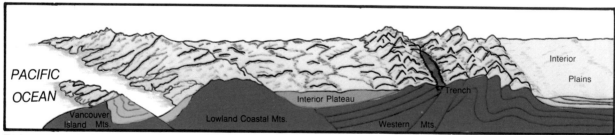

FIGURE 8: A view across the cordillera.

What is the climate like on the cordillera?

There are a number of different climates in the cordilleran region. Within very short distances the temperature and rainfall may vary. Even as you travel from valley to mountain top you may pass through a number of different climates. Coastal temperatures are warmer than those inland. Northern climates are cooler than southern.

In the north winters may last up to eight months. They are cold and long. In the south winters may be quite different from place to place because of the mountains.

The amount of rain that falls also depends on where people live. It may rain very heavily along the coast. Some of the southern valleys inland are often very dry.

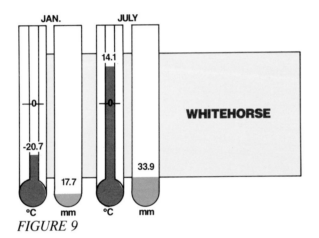

FIGURE 9

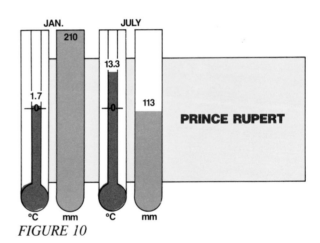

FIGURE 10

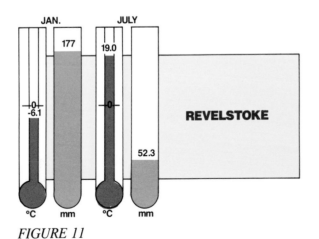

FIGURE 11

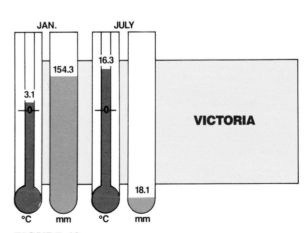

FIGURE 12

Average temperatures only give part of the information about the climate in a place. The averages have been kept over many years. There may be great differences from year to year.

The daily and seasonal weather may change greatly. Wind storms often lash the West Coast and are a danger for fishers and boat traffic.

Rainstorms may cause rivers to flood their banks and damage homes and property.

Too little rain can cause **droughts**. This weather may dry the forests and raise the danger of forest fires.

FIGURE 13: Victoria, B.C.

Read the Charts

1. What are the average daily January and July temperatures in your community?
2. Which place given in the charts has temperatures closest to those of your community?
3. Write a sentence comparing winter and summer temperatures on the cordillera.
4. Which place given on the charts probably has the longest growing season?
5. Do the charts give enough information about the climate of each place to help someone decide whether or not it would be a comfortable place to live?

Weather Events

Think about the temperatures on your own birthday. How have they varied over the years? What would you guess has been the average temperature on your birthday?

Using the Information

1. Try to find out what the weather has been like on your birthday for the past five years. Does this information agree or disagree with what you have just read?
2. What is an "average"?
3. Copy the following chart into your notebook and complete it.

	Kinds of weather	Effect
◯		

FIGURE 14

25

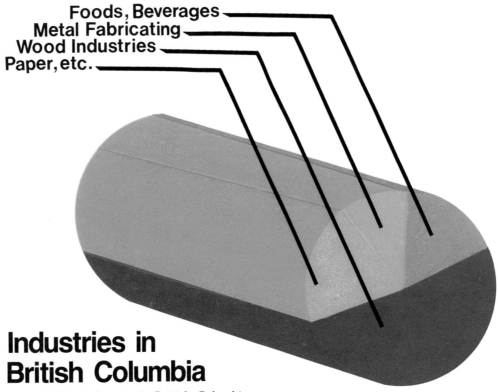

Foods, Beverages
Metal Fabricating
Wood Industries
Paper, etc.

Industries in British Columbia

FIGURE 15: Industries in British Columbia.

What resources are found on the cordillera?

The cordillera has many natural resources. Forests cover much of the region. There are two kinds of forests on the cordillera and their trees are used differently. Coastal forests have been used to make pulp and paper. Inland forests have been used mostly for lumber.

Fish are gathered along the West Coast. Most canneries are located near the mouths of two rivers, the **Fraser** and the **Skeena**.

Mines are found across the region, with the most activity around the city of **Trail**, British Columbia. There are rich deposits of minerals, which could be mined, in **Yukon**. However, there are fewer mines here because of the high cost of transporting material to markets.

The beautiful mountains make the cordillera an attractive playground for tourists and people interested in recreation.

Read the Graph

1. What does the graph describe?
2. Upon what other industries does construction depend?
3. Does the graph tell you which are the most important industries? Why?

Harvesting Forests

How many trees should be cut from cordilleran forests? Some Canadians say none. These people often live in cities. They want to see forests left wild for people to enjoy. Others feel that with wise planning we can conserve our forests while harvesting what we need.

Without careful planning the results can be bad. When too many trees are cut in one patch there have been landslides. The soils may be washed away in places. Streams may be clogged with left-over branches and logs. When this happens fish may die. Animal homes and food may be destroyed. Care must be taken when logging roads are built or the same things may happen.

Before logging begins, planners think about questions such as:

1. What roads will be needed? How can they be built to cause little damage to the land?
2. What methods will be used to cut the trees?
3. How large a patch will be cut? In **Alaska** loggers cannot cut down more than 40 hectares in one patch or strip of some kinds of trees.
4. How will the trees be stored or piled once they are cut?
5. How will streams be protected?
6. How will trees be moved to sawmills?
7. How will fires be controlled?
8. How can they make sure the forest will grow back in the cut patches?

FIGURE 16: Which areas have been logged?

FIGURE 17: How have chain saws helped loggers?

FIGURE 18: Why is the logging area kept clean?

FIGURE 19: How does this machine improve logging?

FIGURE 20: List the items made from wood.

A Problem to Ponder

Should logging be allowed in National Parks?

FIGURE 21

A Stock of Fish

The fishing grounds of the cordillera region are the shallow waters along the coast. Fish live here eating the very **minute** plant and animal life which are found in the water. These animals and plants are called **plankton.**

Salmon, herring, and halibut are the main fish caught. Salmon is the most important as sixty cents out of every dollar earned from the catch comes from these fish.

Salmon are caught in the summer. There are different kinds of salmon and they are used differently. **Sockeyes, pinks,** and **chums** are canned. **Cohos** are sold fresh, smoked and frozen. The largest are called **chinooks**. They are sold fresh or frozen.

FIGURE 22: A halibut boat.

FIGURE 23: *The Fowler family.*

The Fowler Family—Halibut Fishers

The Talbot family spent part of one summer vacation in **Prince Rupert** visiting friends. There they met the Fowler fishing crew.

The Fowler family owns a halibut fishing boat. It is a fairly large boat and can carry enough fuel to travel over twelve hundred kilometres. Six fishers can sleep on the boat. It can carry enough supplies for the crew to fish for about ten days at a time. The boat has a radio-telephone and a **depth-sounder** to help find fish.

The halibut are caught by a way of fishing called **long lining**. Short, light, fishing lines baited with herring are attached to a heavier line. Anchors hold the line in place so it will not be moved by ocean currents. **Buoys** and floats mark the line.

A winch hauls the line with the caught halibut back to the boat. Here the fish are cleaned and packed in ice. When storage space for fish on the boat is filled, the crew returns to Prince Rupert.

At Prince Rupert the fish are graded and sold to a buyer. Some of the fish may be repacked in ice and sent to cities in Canada. A large part of the catch is usually frozen and placed in storage.

Using the Information

1. What kinds of fish are caught on the West Coast of Canada?
2. What is the most important kind of fish caught?
3. What methods are used to catch fish?
4. What problems might the Fowler fishing crew face?

A Storehouse of Minerals

The history of the cordillera is filled with stories of gold rushes. In 1859 gold was found in the **Cariboo**, the name given to the country in the **Fraser River Valley** north of **Cache Creek.** Stories are told of people like Billy Barker who became rich overnight from the gold he took from his **claim** there.

Dawson City, Yukon, was once the largest city in Canada west of **Winnipeg** thanks to gold. When gold was discovered in the **Bonanza Creek**, John Ladue staked out a town at the mouth of the **Klondike River.** Soon he was rich, not from gold, but from selling lots in his new town of Dawson City.

Today gold is still important but many other minerals are also mined on the cordillera. They may be grouped into three classes: minerals for making metals, minerals for construction, and mineral fuels.

These minerals are used on the cordillera and sold to other parts of Canada and the world. Coal from British Columbia is sold by a special arrangement to **Ontario.** Huge amounts are also sold to **Japan** where the cost of transporting the coal is more than the cost of the coal itself.

1980

_____SILVER

____COPPER

_____GOLD

_____LEAD

FIGURE 24: _Value of minerals mined in Yukon—1980. List the minerals in order of their value._

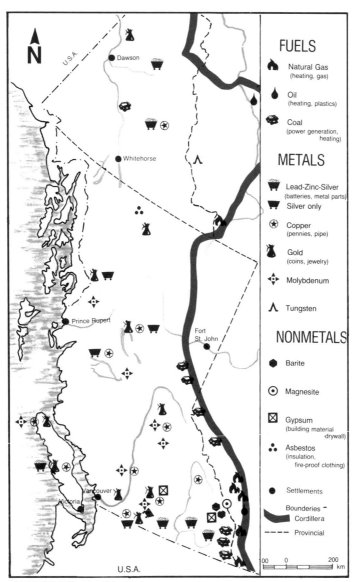

FIGURE 25: *Cordilleran resources and major centres.*

Read the Map

1. What is shown on the map?
2. In what part of the Canadian cordillera are most mines found?
3. Name the major centres closest to lead and zinc mines.
4. Sketch the symbols used on the map in your notebook.

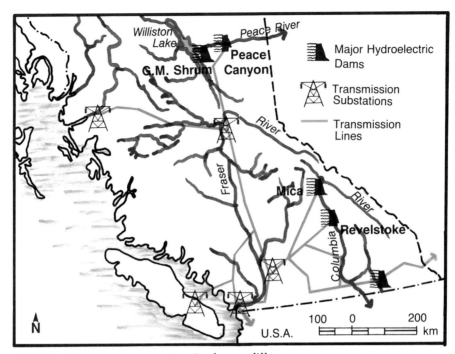

FIGURE 26: Major power sites in the cordillera.

Powerful Water:

A mountain landscape and heavy rains has made many fast flowing rivers on the cordillera. Many of these are used to make electricity. In fact, most of the electricity used in British Columbia is **hydro-electricity.**

Not all the rivers which would be good for making electricity can be used. Some are too far away from settlements to transport the power at a reasonable cost. Dams on others would ruin the rivers for salmon which come there to lay their eggs. Because some of the rivers flow across the border into the United States, damming them could cause problems.

FIGURE 27: Seven Mile power dam southeast of Trail, B.C.

A Beautiful Environment

Snow-capped mountains, clean lakes, racing waterways, long coastlines, and a restless ocean make up an environment which people come from all over the world to visit. This is another of the natural resources of the cordillera.

Travellers come from other parts of Canada, the United States, Japan, **Britain**, and Europe to share this resource. Camping, hiking, sightseeing, boating, and just relaxing keep them busy. Most of these tourists spend their time in southwestern British Columbia. Others, however, head north for adventure at

Kluane Park in Yukon or to relive gold rush days in Dawson City.

To save the environment for the future and for people to enjoy, many parks have been set aside on the cordillera. There are five national parks in British Columbia alone, and there are hundreds of provincial parks.

Many of the tourists found in these parks are the people who live on the cordillera. The Talbot family is similar to many who love to travel around their region. They will travel Trans Canada Highway #1 this summer when they spend a week camping in **Yoho National Park.**

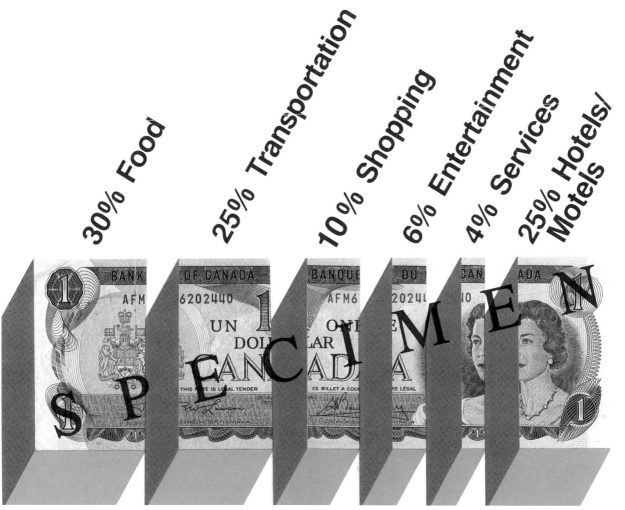

FIGURE 28: On which three items do tourists spend the most money?

FIGURE 29: How is Vancouver like your community? different?

Where do people live?

People live in many different kinds of settlements in the cordillera. They vary from small towns along the highways, ranches among the mountains, mining towns such as Trail, small cities such as Whitehorse, to the large city of Vancouver.

The region is very large, yet almost seven out of ten people live within 120 kilometres of the city of Vancouver. People live on a very, very small part of the land of the cordillera.

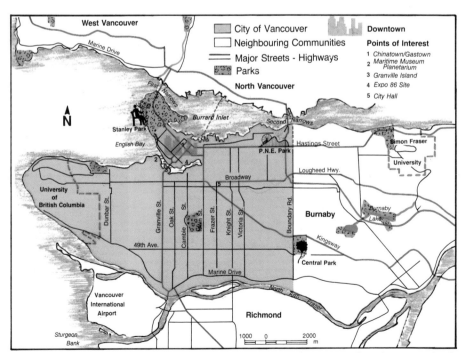

FIGURE 30: Which of the places on the map can you locate in the photograph above?

Vancouver: A coastal city

The Talbot family live within walking distance of Stanley Park in Vancouver. Members of their family have lived in this city since the first sawmill was built along **Burrard Inlet** in 1862.

The city first grew around Burrard Inlet but it has spread and grown to the lower slopes of the **Coast Mountains** to the north. The harbour is deep enough to hold the world's largest ships.

The Talbot family is very fond of their city. They believe that its location near the mountains and ocean make it one of the most beautiful cities in the world. They know that the mild summers make it a very comfortable place to live.

Often family and friends from other parts of Canada visit the Talbots. The Talbots love to show people their city. One place they always take visitors to see is **Stanley Park**. Just over 400 hectares in size, Stanley Park is world famous.

Starting at **Georgia Street** they drive toward **Brockton Point.** Along the way they stop at lookout points for fine views of the harbour. Just before they reach the point they stop to look at the totem poles built by West Coast Indians.

At **Prospect Point** they often watch large ships pass through **First Narrows** under the **Lion's Gate Bridge.**

As they continue along the drive, they are inland and surrounded by huge trees. They often stop and follow the path to the seawall and a view of **Siwash Rock.**

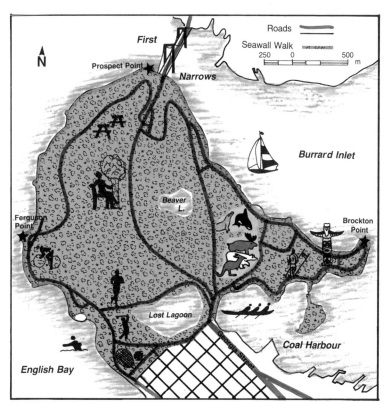

FIGURE 31: Stanley Park.

FIGURE 32: Brockton Point.

FIGURE 33: Stanley Park.

FIGURE 34: Ship sailing under Lion's Gate Bridge.

FIGURE 35: University of British Columbia.

At **Ferguson Point** they are able to point to the **University of British Columbia** on **Point Grey Peninsula**, to **Third Beach**, and on a clear day to the mountains on **Vancouver Island**.

Before they leave the park they always stop to visit the zoo and the aquarium.

As they show visitors their city, the Talbots talk about why it has become the third largest **metropolitan area** in Canada.

Indians first lived in the area. **Captain George Vancouver** explored Burrard Inlet as part of his travels along the West Coast in 1791. In 1808 **Simon Fraser** ended his journey where the city now stands.

Settlers began to arrive in the area in 1862. Most of them lived around **Coal Harbour** on Burrard Inlet. Settlement continued to

FIGURE 36: Where in Stanley Park would this picture be taken?

grow quickly, especially when a brickyard was opened in 1882. Soon sawmills were opened on both sides of Burrard Inlet. People came to set up businesses to serve the workers in the brickyard and sawmills.

It was when the **Canadian Pacific Railway** decided that this place would be the end of the railway line they had built across Canada that the city was really born. By 1886 there were 2000 people living there. That year it was declared a city and was renamed Vancouver. One month later, the land for Stanley Park was set aside for public use.

Read the Map

1. What direction did the Talbots travel as they drove down Georgia Street to Stanley Park?
2. Make a list of recreation activities available in the park.
3. Which bodies of water surround Stanley Park?
4. About how wide is the park from Ferguson Point to Brockton Point?
5. Make a key which would explain the symbols used on this map.

Using the Information

1. Why was a settlement started on Burrard Inlet?
2. Make a short timeline for Vancouver.
3. How does Stanley Park make Vancouver a better city?
4. How many hectares is your school yard? About how many times larger than your school yard is Stanley Park?

FIGURE 37: The Martell family.

How do people earn a living?

The Martell Family

Mr. Martell: "I am retired now. My wife, Hilda, and I moved to **Kamloops**, British Columbia, last summer. We had a large home in **Edmonton** which we sold to buy the house trailer in which we now live.

"Many people move to British Columbia when they retire. We picked Kamloops because it is one of the sunniest cities in Canada.

"Before we retired both Hilda and I taught school. Now that we no longer work we are able to live on our **pension** money."

Mrs. Martell: "Since we moved from Edmonton I have had bad luck with my health. I dislike having to use crutches or a wheelchair. I find it especially annoying to have to ask my husband to help me every time I want to go somewhere.

"We buy most of the things we need right here in Kamloops. Every once in a while we drive south to the United States and do some shopping. We also look forward to trips to Vancouver."

The Stillman Family

"Since my husband and I were divorced, I have lived with my daughter in a high-rise apartment in Vancouver. I own a small bookshop in the downtown part of the city. We do not make a lot of money at the store, but we are certainly not poor.

"The tourists make a big difference to my business. We carry a wide selection of materials about British Columbia just for them."

FIGURE 39: Mrs. Stillman.

FIGURE 38: Cheryl Stillman.

"My name is Cheryl. I am in my last year of high school. I attended a private school in the northern part of Vancouver.

"I am really becoming a history fan. I think I've read every history book that Mom has in the store. When I finish high school, I hope to go to university and study more history. My secret ambition is to write a history of Canada for young children—one with many pictures and few dates!"

FIGURE 40: Mr. Aoki.

FIGURE 41: Mrs. Aoki.

FIGURE 42: George Aoki.

The Aoki Family

Mr. Aoki: "I am a construction worker. I have worked to help build shopping centres, houses. apartments, and schools. Most of the time I have worked within driving distance of our home here in Vancouver. I enjoy construction work very much. I like to work outdoors. It keeps me healthy."

George Aoki: "I find my job as an engineer very interesting. I guess I was first interested in engineering when I visited my Dad on construction jobs. I would watch as huge steel beams were put in place, or concrete was poured, and wonder who did all the planning to make sure the building was strong enough.

"I have worked on projects all over the province. The largest was the building of the **Peace River Power Project**."

Mrs. Aoki: "I have been selling real estate for five years. It is a job I enjoy very much. Unfortunately, there have not been a lot of buyers for the kinds of homes I like to sell — larger and older homes. Even so, I have been able to reach my target each month."

FIGURE 43: The Rochtford family.

The Rochtford Family

"We own a fruit farm in the **Okanagan Valley**. Our farm is almost fourteen hectares in size. We grow peaches on almost eleven hectares of our land along with one hectare each of cherries and apricots.

"Each year at picking time we have to hire people to help us with the orchard. Most of the year we have one or two extra workers to help with irrigating, spraying, and other farm jobs."

Using the Information

1. List the jobs people in these four families do.
2. Place the jobs in two groups:
   Group One:
   People who work with people
   Group Two:
   People who work with things
3. What central place does each family live in or close to?

How are goods moved in the cordillera region?

How do you move shiploads of cars from Japan delivered to Vancouver to other parts of Canada? How do you move the truck loads of wheat from prairie farms to Pacific ports for shipment to **Asia**? Moving goods and people between places in the cordillera and to other parts of Canada can be very difficult.

Canadians have built railways to move large bulky loads. Laying tracks for these trains through the mountains was hard work. The cost in lives and money has been great.

In the 1880s a rail line was built from **Calgary**, Alberta, to Vancouver, British Columbia. It followed river valleys and crossed the **Selkirk Mountains** through **Rogers Pass.**

While these mountains are beautiful to look at, they caused the railway builders many problems. Laying tracks over Rogers Pass

FIGURE 45: *Trans-Canada Highway at Rogers Pass.*

FIGURE 44: *Clearing snow from train tracks in the cordillera region.*

was especially difficult.

Snowfall in the pass is close to ten metres a year. **Avalanches** raced down the slopes at speeds up to 300 kilometres per hour. Workers and equipment were swept along to the valley bottom. **Snowsheds** had to be built over the rails in places where avalanches happened most often. So many workers and equipment were lost that an 8 kilometre tunnel was built below the **summit** through **Mount Mcdonald** in 1916.

Over the last hundred years rail traffic has greatly increased. By the late 1980s as many as fifteen westbound trains a day will use the Rogers Pass. All this traffic means that new railway tracks have had to be built. New tunnels have been dug to avoid the steep slopes, which trains often had to have the help of pusher locomotives to climb.

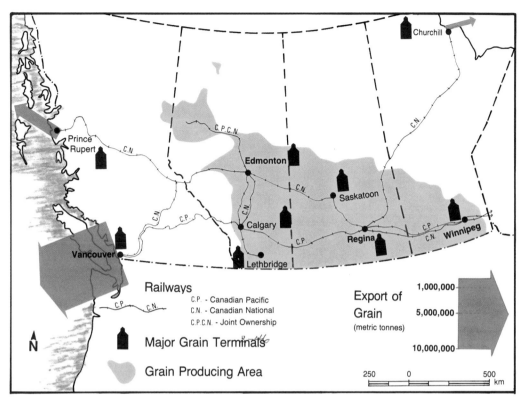

FIGURE 46: Grain producing areas and ports.

Moving prairie grain to cordillera ports

Farms on the Canadian prairies grow grain which is sold to other countries. This grain must be moved from these inland farms to ocean **ports.**

Farmers load grain into trucks which take it to grain **elevators.**

At the elevator it is given a weight, given a grade, and stored in bins.

The grain is next loaded into **hopper cars.**

Grain trains then begin the long trip from the prairies to cordillera grain ports.

There may be delays as the trains cross the mountainous cordillera.

Spring and winter are the worst seasons.

At ports like Vancouver and Prince Rupert, the grain is loaded into **grain terminal elevators.**

The grain is then loaded onto ships. These **merchant vessels** then carry the grain to customers such as China and Japan.

FIGURE 47

FIGURE 48

Moving grain from farm to port.

FIGURE 49

FIGURE 50

Read the Map

1. List the towns the grain train would pass through travelling from **Lethbridge**, Alberta to Vancouver, British Columbia.
2. What is the main direction the train travels once it reaches Calgary?
3. List the boundaries shown on the map.
4. A straight line is the shortest distance between two points. Why is the railway not built in a straight line between Calgary and Vancouver?
5. Why is it difficult to use the map scale to find the distance the train travels from Calgary to Vancouver?

FIGURE 53

FIGURE 51

FIGURE 54

FIGURE 52

Using the Information

1. List the problems which faced railway builders in the cordillera region.
2. Write three newspaper headlines telling about avalanche accidents in the mountains.
3. How else might prairie grain be shipped to customers in Asia?
4. What might happen if grain trains are delayed?
5. Match the information on page 45 with each sketch.

Unit 3

Over Prairie and Plain

What are the interior plains of Canada like?

The interior plains of Canada have the high **Canadian Rocky Mountains** as their western

boundary. On the east and their north the **Canadian Shield** marks the edge. The United States boundary is on the south.

When people think of the plains they usually think of scenes of **prairie** grass blowing in the wind. However, only a small part of this plain is covered with prairie grassland.

Many people believe the plains are almost all flat, level land. This is not true. Although

FIGURE 1

FIGURE 2

List the things you see in figures 1, 2, 3, & 4. Which things seem to belong together?
Write a sentence based on the groups you have made which tells about the plains region.

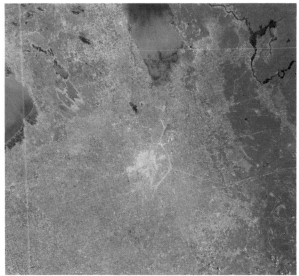

FIGURE 3

FIGURE 4

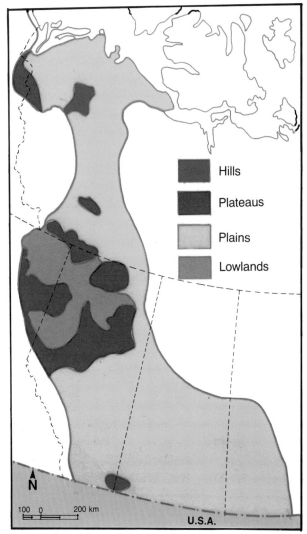

FIGURE 5: Map of the interior plains.

half of the area is very flat, there are many different landscapes. Hills, wide river valleys, **escarpments**, and even low mountains are found on the plains.

Geographers have used a number of ways of looking at the plains region. One is shown in Figure 6. It shows the region divided into three prairie levels.

These three levels are outlined on page 51.

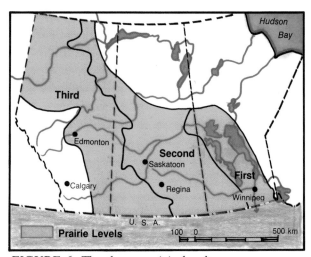

FIGURE 6: The three prairie levels.

FIRST PRAIRIE LEVEL

Land:

• In the south the land is flat.

• Very good soil for growing plants.

• It is believed that this land was once covered by *Lake Aggassiz*, a lake formed by melting glacier ice.

• In the north the soil is not quite as good for growing plants. **Marshland** and wet soils are found here.

Drainage:

• *Drained by the* **Red River** *in the south.*

SECOND PRAIRIE LEVEL

Land:

• Large flat areas of land.

• In the west there are **moraines**, deposits of sand and gravel, which it is believed were left during the ice age.

Drainage:

• *Rivers have deep wide valleys. It is believed these river valleys were cut out by melting waters from the ice age glaciers rather than from rivers found in the valleys today.*

THIRD PRAIRIE LEVEL

Land:

• Different kinds of landscapes are found. The **Cypress Hills** and **Wood Mountains** stand above the plain. The **Badlands** of Alberta are also found here.

Drainage:

• *A variety of creeks, ponds, and marshy areas are found in the northern parts. The dry areas of southern Alberta require irrigation for some crops.*

Using the Information

1. Sketch a map of the interior plains in your notebook.
2. List some ways the three prairie levels are the same; different.
3. List the provinces which are part of the interior plains.
4. Write sentences which describe prairie land.
5. What is the difference between prairie and plain?

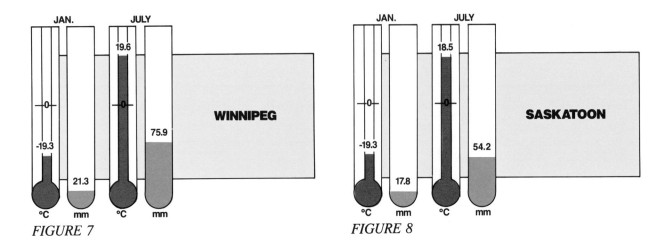

FIGURE 7

FIGURE 8

Temperature and rain/snowfall charts.

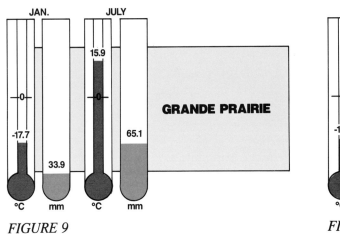

FIGURE 9

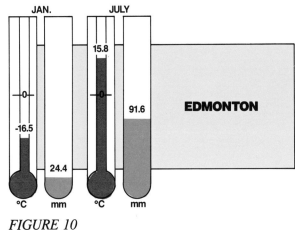

FIGURE 10

What is the climate like on the interior plains?

Temperatures and precipitation may be quite different as you travel from place to place on the plains. The above charts show the climate information for a number of centres.

Read the Charts

1. How are the temperatures for the cities shown the same? How are they different?
2. Do the most northerly cities have the coldest winters? Can you find out why or why not?

FIGURE 11: Weather is very important to people living on the plains.

Temperature and precipitation charts tell only part of the story about the climate of the interior plains. Some years there may be very little precipitation. This causes problems for farmers. Their crops depend upon enough moisture to grow. When it rains very little over a long period of time, it is known as a **drought**.

During a drought fields dry up and plants die. If there are winds, the soil may be blown away. During the 1930s there was a drought on the interior plains. Poet Anne Marriott tells what it was like on a farm at that time:

WIND
In a lonely laughterless shrill game
with broken wash-boiler, bucket without
a handle, Russian thistle, throwing up
sections of soil.

God, will it ever rain again? What about those clouds out west? No, that's just dust, as thick and stifling now as winter underwear. No rain, no crop, no feed, no faith, only wind.

*From: Anne Marriott, **The Wind Our Enemy**. quoted in Green et al. **A Century of Canadian Literature**. pp. 196-197. Toronto: McGraw-Hill Ryerson.*

The wind that poet Marriott talks about is important. How comfortable it is to live in a place depends in part on the temperature and precipitation. It also depends on the amount of wind.

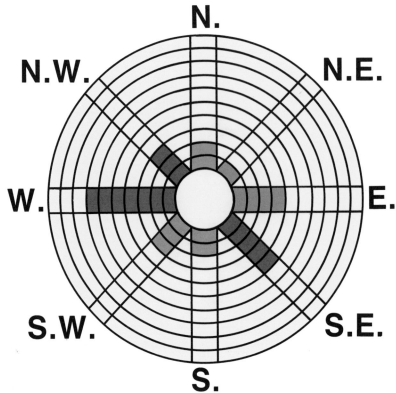

FIGURE 12: The Wind Rose.

Wind Rose

The wind rose has eight arms. Each arm stands for one direction. The arm shows the direction the wind blew from.

Each ring stands for 10% of the time that the wind blew from each direction.

These colours show the average wind speed per hour.

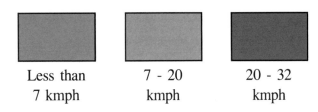

| Less than 7 kmph | 7 - 20 kmph | 20 - 32 kmph |

This wind rose is for a town on the plains. When, for example, the wind blew from **The North**, the average speed was 7 - 20 kmph 20% of the time.

Using the Information

1. Find out the wind information for your community.
2. In what ways does poet Marriott think the wind is in a game?
3. How do we know that she has not lost hope that it will rain?

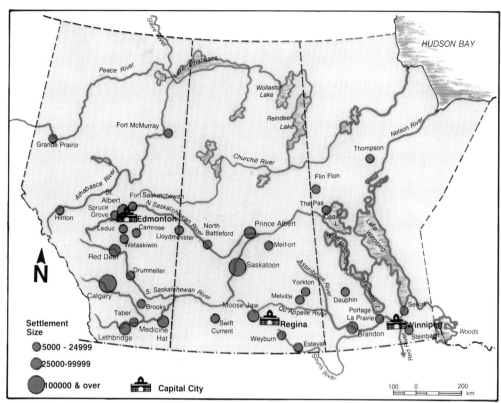

FIGURE 13: Plains population map.

Where do people live on the plains?

Changing Patterns

Most people on the plains live in five cities—Winnipeg, **Regina, Saskatoon,** Edmonton, Calgary—a number of other smaller cities, and large towns. The rest live in smaller towns, villages, and on farms.

Winnipeg is a special city on the plains. Before the railway it was the focus of activity for the region. Settlers entered the region through Winnipeg. The wheat they grew on their farms was shipped to Winnipeg for selling. It was truly the gateway to the west. Places like Edmonton were only small fur trading forts.

Read the Map

1. What does this map show?
2. List the cities of the plains region.
3. Where are most settlements located? Why?

A Problem to Ponder

Selling farmland so that it may be used for factories, houses, or to build roads on has some people worrried. What do you think?

Cities must grow. They cannot be stopped. There is plenty of land in Canada. We don't need to worry about the little used for new communities or factories.

We can help you stop pollution if we use land close to cities for new communities. People living in them will not have to travel so far to get to work.

There is plenty of land on which crops cannot grow. That is the kind of land which should be used to build factories on. Besides it would cost much less than land close to the city.

Most cities grew up on or near land which is good for farming. Some of our very best land for growing crops is being taken away and paved over!

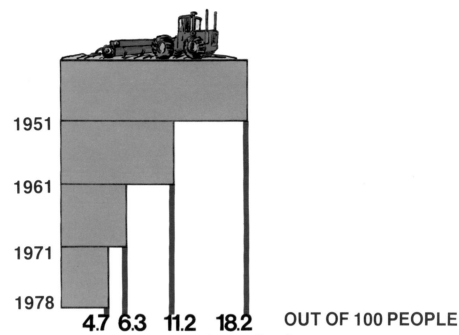

				OUT OF 100 PEOPLE
1951				
1961				
1971				
1978				
4.7	**6.3**	**11.2**	**18.2**	

FIGURE 14: People working in agriculture in Canada.

Read the Graph

1. What does the graph tell?
2. How many workers out of 100 worked in agriculture each year shown?
3. Write a **generalization** which tells about jobs in the plains region.

Over the years there has been a change in the kinds of work people living on the plains do. Look at the information shown in the graph in Figure 14. Over the years fewer and fewer people have worked in farm jobs. Many more people today work in **service jobs.**

Most of these jobs are found in larger communities.

Since your grandparents were born, there has been a change in where people live on the plains. There has been a large movement of people to bigger communities.

People have moved from farms and small communities to larger towns and cities. They have moved for many reasons. New kinds of machinery have made it possible for fewer farmers to do the work of many. Those who are looking for work find a large number of service jobs in cities. Some want to live where they are close to stores and services such as schools, libraries, museums, and hospitals.

There are fewer small communities for a number of reasons. Most families now have dependable cars. Roads which are open all year-round make it possible to travel to all parts of the region. This has made it easy for country dwellers to travel past closer small towns to larger communities. In these large towns or cities they find all the different kinds of stores and services they need.

There are fewer and fewer reasons for them to visit smaller communities. Besides stores, small schools have been closed and big schools have been built in larger communities. Hospitals, government offices, and railway stations are now usually found only in large centres. It is estimated that a trade centre with less than 30 different kinds of stores and services will become smaller in the future.

Using the Information

1. Where does your family shop and do business? Make a list of the businesses and services that your family needs. Where are these stores and services located?
2. State two ways people in a small town might feel about the town becoming smaller.
3. Why do some farm people travel to larger centres to shop when they know that it may help close businesses in a smaller, nearer town?

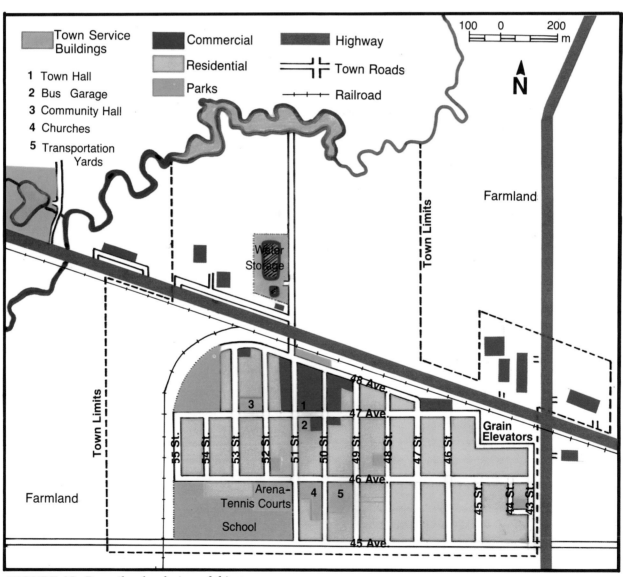

FIGURE 15: Describe the design of this town.

A Visit to Winnipeg—
An Urban Area

Last summer the Lorimer family took their visiting cousins from **Montreal** on a tour of Winnipeg. After the trip they sent this scrapbook page they had prepared to their cousins.

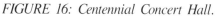
FIGURE 16: Centennial Concert Hall.

FIGURE 17: Zoo, Assiniboine Park.

FIGURE 18: Corner, Portage & Main.

A page from the Lorimer family's scrapbook.

FIGURE 19: Legislative Building.

FIGURE 20: Royal Canadian Mint.

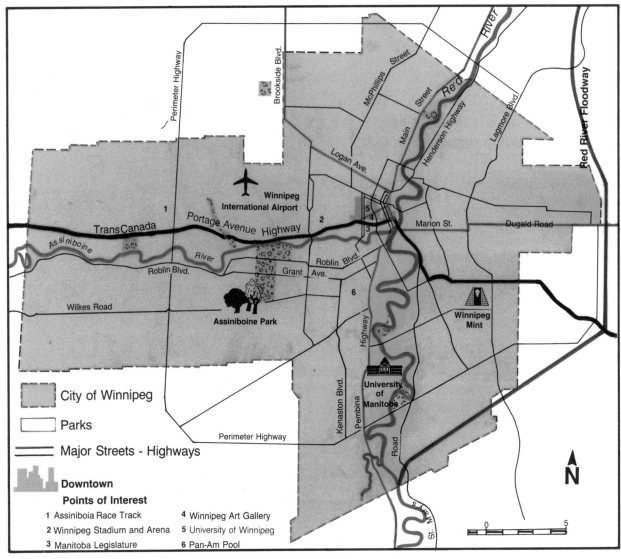

FIGURE 21: Winnipeg, Manitoba.

Read the Map

1. What is the title of the map?
2. Name the rivers which flow through the city
3. How many river bridges are there in the city?
4. What direction is the business district from the airport?

5. If you were travelling west on Highway #1 coming into Winnipeg, how could you avoid the downtown traffic?
6. Write a sentence about how the land Winnipeg is built on affects the transportation routes.
7. Explain how you would travel from the airport to each of the places shown on page 59.

FIGURE 22: How have farms changed since this house was built?

Fewer people—the rural plains

When settlers first came to western Canada they moved onto 64.8 hectare(160 acre) farms. Families owned these farms. These family farms were passed down from parents to children. For many reasons it has become harder and harder to earn enough money on a small family farm to keep a family. Many of these farms have been sold. Some family farmers have had to take another job to make enough money, while still looking after their farms.

Other farm people have moved to cities. They moved to take up different jobs or to enjoy a different way of life and this has made their land available for people to buy. Figure 14 shows how the number of people in Canada working on farms has changed.

Farms are getting larger. There are a number of reasons why this has happened. Where fields were once plowed by a farmer and a team of horses, they are now plowed by huge tractors pulling many plows. Where fields were first cut by horse-drawn **binders,** then **stooked,** and then **threshed,** they are now quickly cut at one time by **self-propelled harvesters.**

FIGURE 23: A scene from the rural plains.

61

FIGURE 24: Many prairie people have moved off their farms to live in big cities. Can you think of any reasons why?

New kinds of farm machinery have been invented. This has meant that now one farmer can do the work of many. It has meant that farmers can now farm much larger farms than in the past. It means that farm products may be raised at less cost than before.

Some of the farms on the prairies have become very large. The size of the average farm has grown. Four hundred and eight hundred hectare farms are now quite common. Some are run by large companies called **corporations.**

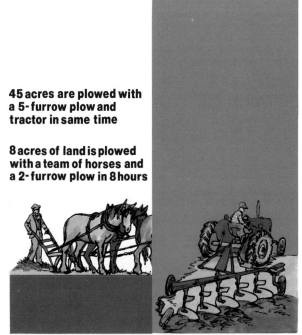

45 acres are plowed with a 5- furrow plow and tractor in same time

8 acres of land is plowed with a team of horses and a 2- furrow plow in 8 hours

FIGURE 25: How does the amount of work done by horse and tractor compare?

FIGURE 26: How has this type of machinery affected farmers?

The Carbdale Grain Company owns such a farm in Manitoba. Their farm is about 1900 hectares. Some of the largest farm machinery which can be bought is used on this farm. There are five trucks, five tractors, and the largest combine that may be purchased in Canada.

Most families do not have the money needed to own and run farms of this size.

They are worried that more and more farms will be bought and run by corporations. They feel that their small farms are in danger. Large farmers are able to farm and sell some products for less. This will make it harder for family farms to make a profit.

Using the Information

1. List three reasons why fewer people live on farms today than in the past.
2. Write a generalization about where people live on the plains.
3. List two things that might be done to help small farmers keep their farms.

FIGURE 27: Hopper cars at a grain elevator.

How do people earn a living?

The soil of the plains region is a valuable natural resource. It is believed that for millions of years grass in the region grew each spring and then died in the fall. This dead grass **decayed** year after year and formed the rich black soil which we now see.

Canada grows grain on this soil which is sold and shipped to people around the world. Wheat is our most important grain crop. It makes us about 10¢ of every $1 that the country receives from **exports**.

The Lorimer Family: Grain Farmers

The Lorimer family own a large wheat farm west of Winnipeg. Like many plains people they earn their living by farming.

The Lorimer family handles all the work on the farm except at harvest time. Then extra people have to be hired to drive trucks and other work which must be done to get the crop off the field. The Lorimers depend on a great deal of modern machinery to do the work on their farm.

Figure 30 shows the year's work on their farm.

FIGURE 28: *The Lorimers' farm.*

FIGURE 29: *The Lorimer family.*

FIGURE 30: A year's work on the Lorimers' farm.

Farmers like the Lorimers face many problems. Hail, which can destroy the crop in minutes, is always feared. Too little rain can cause the crops to dry up and die. And sometimes frosts ruin a crop. Large farm machinery costs a lot of money to buy.

However, even with these possible problems, the family loves to farm. They love the freedom and freshness of living in the country. They are proud of the fine crops they have raised most years on their farm. Providing food for Canadians and people elsewhere is an important job.

THE FARMSTEAD

1. House	7. Granaries	13. Vegetable garden
2. Storage	8. Water pump	14. Potatoes
3. Garage	9. Propane	15. Idle
4. Shop	10. Fuel	16. Shelter belt, trees
5. Barn	11. Grain storage	17. Lilac bushes
6. Chicken coop	12. Kitchen garden	18. Hedge

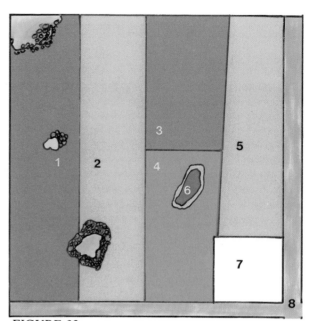

FIGURE 32

THE FARM

1. Summer fallow	4. Pasture	7. Farmstead
2. Wheat	5. Wheat	8. Roads
3. Summer fallow	6. Dugout pond	

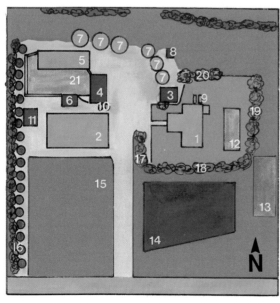

FIGURE 31

Read the Maps

1. **Summer fallow** is land that is allowed a rest from having crops grown on it. This allows moisture and minerals to build up again in the soil. About how much of the Lorimer farm is in summer fallow?
2. The crops are planted in strips to help stop the wind from blowing the soil away. Which direction do you think the wind usually blows from on the Lorimer farm? Why?
3. Why are rows of trees planted around different parts of the farmstead?
4. Why is some land left idle on the farmstead?
5. List the buildings found on the farm. What is each used for?

66

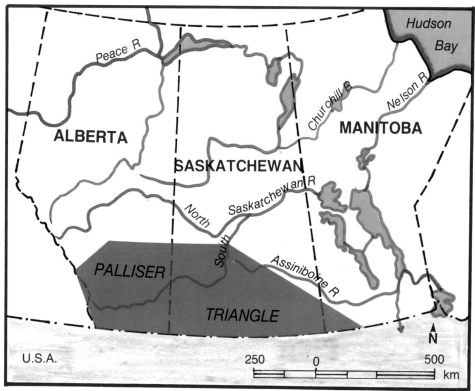

FIGURE 33: The Palliser Triangle.

The Jamieson Family Farm

Part of the plains region was thought to be too dry for crops to be grown. This land is in southern Alberta and Saskatchewan. It is called the **Palliser Triangle**. It is roughly a triangle of land named after the British explorer Captain John Palliser. He wrote: "this...district...can never be much use to us as a possession."

Through the use of irrigation, farmers have proven Captain Palliser to be wrong. A number of dams, **reservoirs,** and a network of irrigation pipelines, canals, and ditches bring water to the land. This allows a number of crops to be raised.

The Jamieson family own and operate an irrigated farm.

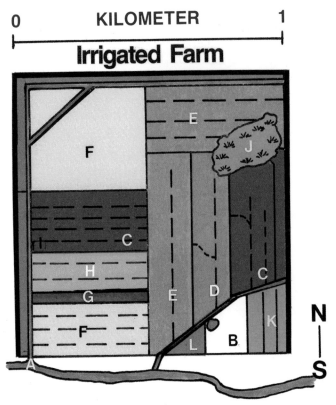

0　KILOMETER　1

Irrigated Farm

FIGURE 34: *This is our farm.*

Their farm is shown in Figure 34. It is located near Lethbridge, Alberta. Carol Lorimer has prepared a report on their farm for social studies class. She used photographs and drawings to illustrate her report.

JAMIESONS' FARM		
A. Irrigation canal	E. Peas	I. Pump
B. Farmstead	F. Wheat	J. Slough
C. Sugar beets	G. Beans	K. Grass
D. Hay	H. Barley	L. Pasture

Read the Map

1. List the crops and animals raised on the farm.
2. List the buildings found on the farm.
3. About how many metres of irrigation ditch are there on the farm?
4. Why is the house located next to the Aspen grove?
5. Which direction would you guess the wind blows from most of the time? Why?

FIGURE 35: *The Jamieson family.*

68

FIGURE 36: "These ditches carry water to our fields."

FIGURE 37: "Irrigated land is flat and makes it possible to move water from place to place."

These are some of the crops we raise on our farm.

FIGURE 38: "These are some of the crops we raise on our farm."

FIGURE 39: "This is our farmstead."

JAMIESONS' FARMSTEAD

A. Farm house
B. Garage
C. Vegetable storehouse
D. Barn
E. Storage bin
F. Hired hands' house
G. Pump house
H. Granaries
I. Molasses stands

J. Propane bins
K. Haystacks
L. Dugout pond
M. Vegetable garden
N. Feedlot
O. Pig pen
P. Corral
Q. Pasture
R. Grass
S. Irrigation Canal

FIGURE 40: Hank Jarvis.

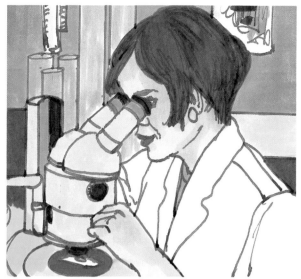

FIGURE 41: Mavis Miller.

FIGURE 42: Marsha Sommers.

FIGURE 43: Don Wright.

Four More Plains Workers

Hank Jarvis is a driller who works in the oil industry. He is a driller who works on rigs searching for new oil.

Mavis Miller is a chemist. She works at a university on a project which is trying to find new ways of making products from oil.

Don Wright is a flight attendant. He works for a large **charter airline** which started as a small company in Edmonton and now flies to many parts of the world.

Marsha Sommers works as a real estate salesperson. Plains cities have known "boom" times when there was plenty of money and property was very valuable. They have also known "busts" when the prices of property dropped. Marsha's company has stayed in business through all this.

FIGURE 44: "YOU CAN BE ANYTHING"— T.V. panel.

These four industry workers are members of a panel being interviewed on television for a series called **You Can Be Anything.** The purpose of the show is to help young Canadians explore the world of work.

HOST: Good Evening. I am Rod Carter, host of our weekly show called, You Can Be Anything.

While driving across the plains, it is not unusual to see oil being pumped from the ground. Sometimes oil rigs are seen at work drilling holes in search of new oil finds. These activities usually take place against a background of farms and fields. One could begin to think of the plains as a world of farm and oil industry workers. There really is much more.

During the next few minutes we will talk to four people involved in different industries on the plains. Through them I hope we will all learn something about the industries in which they work.

Mavis, you're a chemist. What kind of work do you do?

MAVIS MILLER: Right now I am working on a project where we are studying the uses of oil. As you know, some clothes are made from fibres made from petroleum. We are looking for ways to make new, stronger fibres. We work as a team and receive money for our project from the government and a large oil company.

ANNOUNCER: Good, and have you found what you are looking for?

MAVIS MILLER: Not yet, but we think that we are on the right track.

ANNOUNCER: Hank, you work in the oil

industry too. But you have quite a different job from Marsha.

HANK JARVIS: *That's right. I'm pleased that people like Marsha are working to find new products from the oil we bring out of the ground. Drilling for oil can be a risky business. We drill many more dry holes than we do wells from which we get oil. It's my business to know all about drilling. How to get a rig in place. Which **drill bits** to use. And, how to keep the drill working through all kinds of different layers of rock.*

ANNOUNCER: *The kind of education needed for your two jobs must be quite different.*

MAVIS MILLER: *Well, I don't know about Hank but I studied mathematics and special sciences called **physics** and **chemistry** in college. I found I also needed to know how to use a computer for most of my work.*

HANK JARVIS: *Well, I suppose our backgrounds aren't too different. I attended college and studied **geology**. What I learned about rocks and how they are made has been very useful to me.*

ANNOUNCER: *I am a little surprised that you went to college, Hank. Do all drillers have the same education?*

HANK JARVIS: *No. It varies. Some people are trained in trade schools to be drillers. Some of the old-timers learned how just from being around oil rigs. However, these days most oil companies want someone with a good educational background.*

ANNOUNCER: *Well, Marsha, I am sure you don't need a college education to sell real estate.*

MARSHA SOMMERS: *You might be surprised. Many real estate salespeople do have a college education. Courses are offered in some colleges. They often attend college*

before entering the real estate business. In addition, all salespeople have to have special training and earn a license to sell real estate.

They have to know something about the law and contracts, they have to learn about buildings and the value of property, and they must learn how to get along with people and work with customers. Like Mavis, most of us have found computers to be very useful tools.

ANNOUNCER: *Well, Don, that leaves you. What kind of things do you study to be a flight attendant?*

DON WRIGHT: *Flight attendants have many different backgrounds. Some airlines will not hire you unless you have studied in college for two years. And, of course, if you are going to be on flights to other countries you must be able to speak the languages that are used there very well.*

What I enjoy most is meeting people, the travel with lots of vacations, and plenty of time off. I usually spend about 80 hours each month flying and 35 hours of ground work.

Because airlines fly all day every day, we work in shifts. This can mean you have an unusual schedule. Delays too can mean you end up working long days.

ANNOUNCER: *Well, there we are—four more jobs. They are all quite different, but in many ways the same. They all need people who have a good level of education. They all need people who are curious about the world around them. And, each job requires some very special skills.*

*There we are then. Four more jobs you can add to your **You Can Be Anything** list. See you next week.*

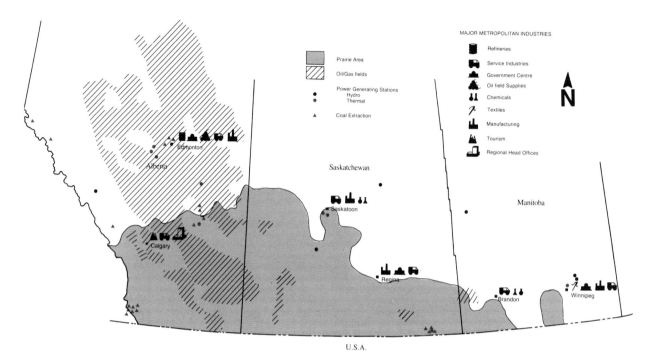

FIGURE 45: Products and industries on the plains.

Using the Information

1. Copy the following chart into your notebook using information from the "You Can Be Anything" television show.

Job	Education Needed	What They Do

2. Here is a list of important industries in Saskatchewan:

    Agriculture
    Forestry
    Fisheries
    Trapping
    Mining
    Electric Power
    Manufacturers
    Construction

    List those which are not found in the plains region of the province.

Read the Map

1. What is shown on the map?
2. List ten industries found on the plains.
3. List five resources the industries shown on the map use.

74

Unit 4

Across the North

Where is the "north"?

Canadians are used to talking about the north. Our country is located in the northern **hemisphere.** People in southern Canada talk incorrectly about "going up north." Even our national anthem **O'Canada** talks about "... the true north strong and free." But what exactly is the north?

For purposes of this chapter we will call the north region that land where there is frost in the ground all year round. As you can see from Figure 5 this region overlaps other regions such as the Cordillera and the Canadian Shield.

An arctic climate, few people, and different kinds of landscapes are found in the region. It stretches from the Atlantic to the Pacific Ocean and includes the Arctic Ocean.

FIGURE 1

FIGURE 2

List the things shown in photographs 1, 2, 3 and 4. Group those items which seem to belong together. Write a sentence on these groups which tells about the north.

FIGURE 3

FIGURE 4

FIGURE 5: Which provinces and territories have permafrost?

Read the Maps

1. List the provinces and territories which have land north of where frost never leaves the ground.
2. List ten of the largest settlements found in the region.
3. List five of the largest islands in the region.
4. What is the distance from Alert to **Tuktoyaktuk**?
5. In what direction would you travel from Alert to Tuktoyaktuk?

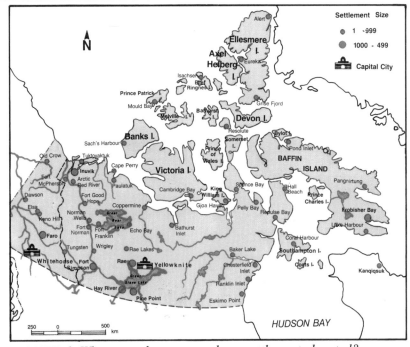

FIGURE 6: Where are the most northern settlements located?

FIGURE 7: What kinds of landscapes are found across the north?

What is the land like across the north?

There are four main kinds of landscapes found across the north. They include lowlands, plateaus, mountains, and ice-cap.

Lowland landscapes

As is shown in Figure 7, there are large areas of low level land with low rounded hills. Much of this land is called **tundra.** In summer some parts are covered with low grass, moss, small bushes, some flowers, and **lichens.** Trees do not grow. Other parts are **barren.** In these places no plants grow.

Low hills, small lakes and swamps, and rocks left behind by the glaciers are found in some places.

Because only the top few inches of ground near the surface thaws each year, the roots of tundra plants do not go very deep. Caribou herds depend on the lichens for food.

FIGURE 8: Tundra lichens.

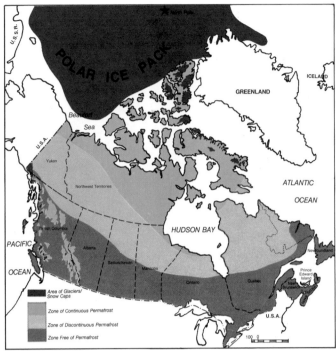

FIGURE 9: What does this map show about the polar ice pack?

Plateau landscapes

The plateau parts of the north are rolling land. Along the ocean these plateaus form high cliffs. The coast has many ravines and **fjords.**

Large parts of the plateaus are barren. They are covered with loose rock and gravel. During a very short time during the summer plants may grow on parts of this barren land.

Other parts of the plateau are covered by tundra.

Mountain landscapes

High mountains with sharp peaks and deep valleys are found in parts of this region. From the air these mountains appear completely covered with snow even in mid-summer. Glaciers fill many valleys and near

the sea these flow into the sea and become **icebergs**.

Ice covered landscape

In the northern part of this region is found an ice cover which never melts. The map in Figure 10 shows the boundary of this ice pack. Surrounding this permanent ice is an area where ships with special ice breaking equipment can travel. They usually travel only between the months of June and September.

FIGURE 10: Satellite image of the polar ice cap from the air.

Using the Information

1. List the four kinds of landscapes found in the north. Use the map given in Figure 7 to describe where each landscape is found.
2. What kind of land is **Inuvik**, shown on page 93, built on?
3. What possible transportation problems does each kind of landscape present?

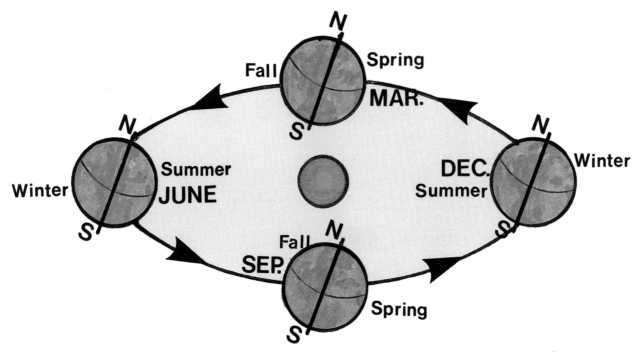

FIGURE 11: a) Place your finger on the word December. Follow the orbit to March, next to June, on to September, and back to December. You have just traced the trip the Earth takes once each year. b) The Earth's axis is tilted. In December the North Pole is tilted away from the sun. The number of hours the North faces the sun each day are few.

What is the climate like in the north?

The movement of the earth around the sun causes seasons. The earth moves around the sun once a year and spins once each day on its **axis**. The axis is tilted and always points into space at the same angle. Figure 11 shows that in Summer the **North Pole** is pointed toward the sun. Six months later, in winter, it points away from the sun.

We know the earth travels around the sun. However, to us the sun appears to move across the sky each day. We say the sun rises in the east and sets in the west. This is called the **apparent path** of the sun.

FIGURE 12: How the sun appears to northerners.

80

Read the Diagram

1. What direction do people look to see the sun?
2. During what month does the sun appear to be highest in the sky?
3. How do these apparent movements of the sun affect the climate?

A Dry Climate

Two large climate regions are found in the north. They are tundra and ice-cap. Rain and snowfall in these regions is light, averaging between 250-360 millimetres a year.

Read the Charts

1. Use your atlas to locate each community.
2. How are the temperatures in the four communities the same? Different?
3. How is the precipitation in the four communities the same? Different?
4. Write a sentence telling about January temperatures in the north.
5. Look at the chart for Inuvik. Write a sentence telling about its temperatures.

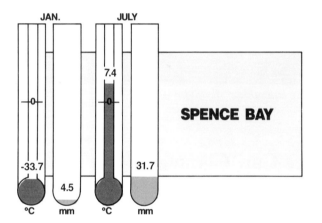

FIGURE 13

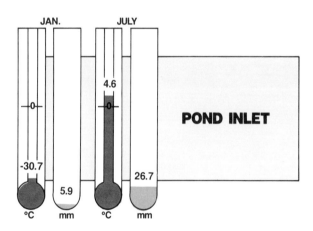

FIGURE 14

Average temperatures, in degrees Celsius and average precipitation, in millimetres, for four northern communities.

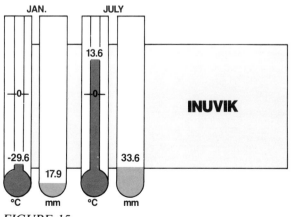

FIGURE 15

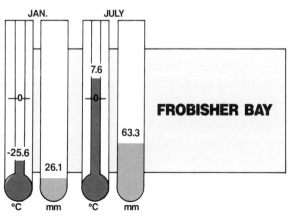

FIGURE 16

FIGURE 17: How is the land different from land in your community? Is it the same?

In tundra regions the climate is too cold and dry for trees to grow. Summers are cool and short. Under the top few inches of soil the ground contains permafrost. Only this top soil melts in summer.

Tundra climates can be quite different from place to place but they are dry. Figure 18 shows the average temperature for Alert.

Alert has a very dry climate. Its total precipitation is made almost entirely of snow. It is very close to being a desert climate.

The sun is never very high in the sky as you move further north. In places like **Lake Hazen**, there is a long winter period when the sun does not rise. Likewise, the sun never sets from April 10 to September 6.

Ice-Cap Climate

Ice caps cover parts of **Ellesmere Island** and **Baffin Island**. It rarely rains, but it may snow any month of the year. The snow which falls turns into ice under its own weight. In general the average temperature stays below freezing all year round. The largest ice-cap in the Arctic is on **Greenland**, one of Canada's northern neighbours.

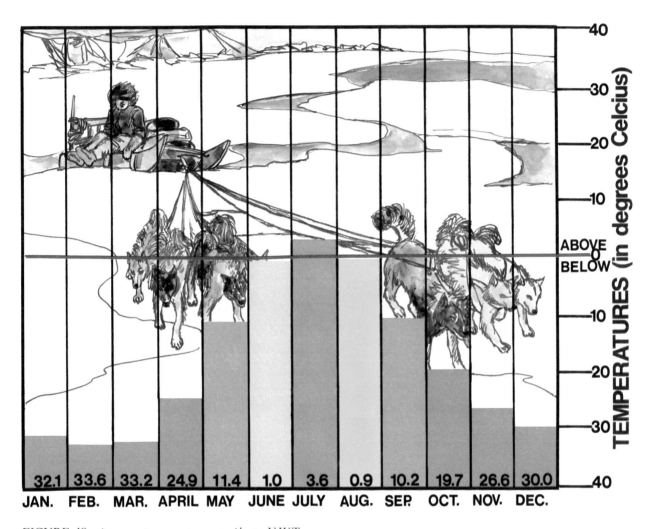

32.1	33.6	33.2	24.9	11.4	1.0	3.6	0.9	10.2	19.7	26.6	30.0
JAN.	FEB.	MAR.	APRIL	MAY	JUNE	JULY	AUG.	SEP.	OCT.	NOV.	DEC.

FIGURE 18: *Average temperature at Alert, N.W.T.*

Using the Information

1. Write a weather report for a January day in Alert.
2. List the equipment airplanes travelling in the north might have to carry because of the climate.

Auyuittuq Park: a National Park north of the Arctic Circle

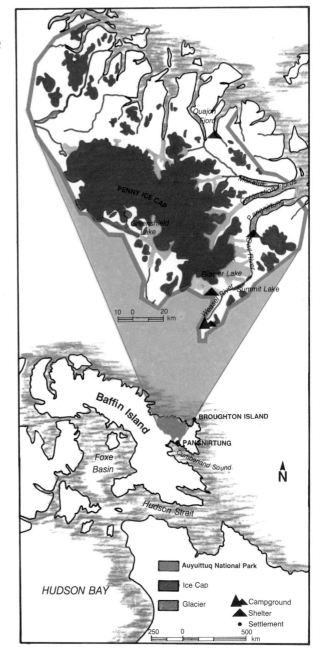

FIGURE 19: Location of Auyuittuq (I-YOU-WE-TOOK) Park, N.W.T.

FIGURE 20: John Otak, Park Ranger.

Auyuittuq (I-YOU-WE-TOOK) National Park was set aside in 1972. This part of Baffin Island has been set aside to save a large area of mountains and fiords. The word auyuittuq is Inuttitut and means "the place which does not melt." It is a wilderness park. To travel to the park most visitors fly from Montreal to **Frobisher Bay** and then to Pangnirtung.

What will you see in our most northerly park? Beautiful mountains, ice-fields, and steep fiords make up the scenery in the park. Hikers will see Arctic hare, Arctic fox, polar bear, caribou, and many lemmings. Ptarmigan, ducks, snowy owls, and falcons will be spied by the very observant. And, water watchers may see whales, narwhals, walrus, and seals in the park's fiords.

The **Penny Ice Cap** which scientists believe is left from the last ice age, covers a large part of the park.

John Otak lives in Pangnirtung on Baffin Island. During the summer he is a park ranger in Auyuittuq National Park. He gives advice to, and helps the 100 to 300 people who come to visit this northern park.

Putting up trail markers, acting as guide, and keeping emergency tourist cabin shelters liveable takes up the rest of his time.

Using the Information

1. What is a wilderness park?
2. Why do Canadians have National Parks?
3. How do rangers help tourists?
4. What damage might visitors do to the park?
5. What might happen if a tourist were not properly prepared for hiking in the park?
6. List the sights a tourist might see. Make a sketch of some of the animals.

Who are the people who live across the north?

Many of the people who live in northern Arctic communities are **Inuit** and **Indian** There are about 24,000 Inuit across this large area of Canada. That means that if all these people were brought together they would fill the seats in a small football stadium.

Often the names one group of people give to another are not very flattering. For years these people were called the Eskimos. It was a name given to them by the Indians and meant "eaters of raw flesh." Inuit leaders have asked that the name be dropped. They want the following words used instead:

When speaking to one person the word to use is **Inuk**.

When speaking of three or more people the word to use is Inuit.

When speaking of their language the word to use is **Inuttitut**.

Inuttitut is so different from English that it is difficult to change words from one language to another. However for now these words seem appropriate.

Early Canadian explorers from Europe first met the Inuit on their travels. But it was the arrival of whaling ships that started to change the way the Inuit lived. By trading with the whalers the Inuit began to depend upon goods from the Europeans. Because Europeans wanted furs, the Inuit changed from hunting and fishing to trapping so they would have furs to trade. They traded these at trading posts which were built across the North. Today the **Hudson's Bay Company** has more than thirty trading posts.

When the early Europeans came to the North they brought with them sickness and disease. Influenza, tuberculosis, and measles sometimes killed whole communities of Inuit.

Across the North other native peoples, the Indians, have a history which is much the same as that of the Inuit. They had to hunt to live. Streams, lakes, and the sea provided fish. Caribou herds and musk-oxen provided meat. When there were no animals to be found people starved.

World War II changed the North for ever. Air travel grew and made it possible for people to get to remote places in the North. Radio and weather stations were built and people from the South came to work in them. For the first time numbers of white people started to live in northern communities.

FIGURE 21: *Brenda and Frank Kannuk.*

Brenda and Frank Kunnuk:
A Trapper Hunter Family

Brenda and Frank Kunnuk and their family live on **Victoria Island** in the Arctic. Their village is one of Inuit hunters and trappers. They are known for the seals, fox, and caribou that they hunt and for the arctic char they catch.

One of the biggest changes that has happened in the village is the use of snowmobiles rather than dog teams by hunters and trappers. A snowmobile can travel 160 to 240 km a day compared to 35-50 km by dog teams. This has meant that, with people living in the villages, hunters are able to hunt and trap hundreds of miles from home. This was important because the animals living near settlements were soon hunted or trapped. Snowmobiles allow the villagers to travel long distances to find the arctic char and caribou they eat.

The Kunnuk family makes their living hunting and trapping. The size of the family changes from year to year. It depends on which

"The first snow comes in early September. I repair machinery and my hunting equipment.

"Our first hunting/trapping trip of the year is to a lake, about 95 km north.

"We catch enough arctic char for our family for the winter months.

*"We hunt **tuktuk**, small caribou, which are fat from summer feeding.*

"I set out 300 to 400 traps. It takes me about two weeks.

"During the winter I spend a week at home and then 7-10 days checking my trapline. The trapping season ends in mid-May.

"Our whole family moves to a summer camp on Iluvilik Island. There we hunt seals and ducks. On trips to nearby lakes we are able to catch trout.

"At the end of August we return to the village. School opens and we return to village life."

FIGURE 22: "The first snow comes in early September. I repair machinery and my hunting equipment."

FIGURE 23: "Our first hunting/trapping trip of the year is to a lake about 95 km north."

FIGURE 24: "We catch enough Arctic char for our family for the winter months."

FIGURE 25: "We hunt tuktuk (small caribou) which are fat from summer feeding."

FIGURE 26: *"I set out 300 to 400 traps. It takes me about two weeks."*

Using the Information

1. List three ways in which the Europeans changed the lives of the Inuit.
2. Give two reasons why Europeans travelled to the Arctic.
3. List the ways in which life for the Kunnuk family is the same as yours. List ways in which it is different.
4. List the inventions which have changed life for the Inuit in the North.

FIGURE 27: *"At the end of August we return. School opens and we return to village life."*

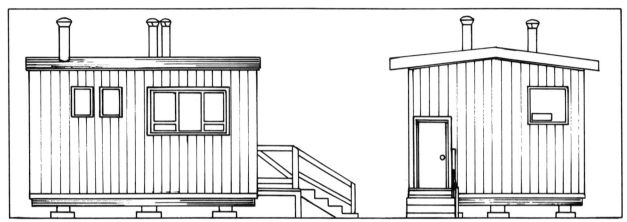

FIGURE 28: How is this northern home similar to your own? Different?

Where do people live?

Houses and other buildings

In most Canadian communities the kinds of buildings which will be built depend only in part upon the environment. Some will have basements, others will not. Different kinds of foundations are built to support buildings. Often it depends on what the buyer wants.

In places where there is always frost in the ground permafrost builders must

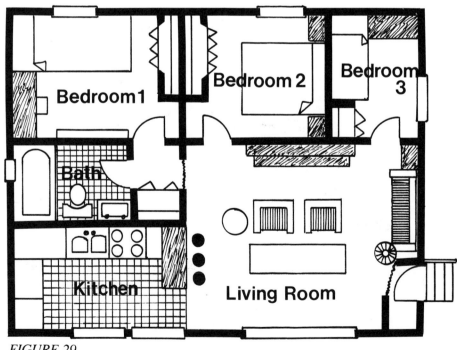

FIGURE 29

FIGURE 30: *What are the advantages of prefabricating a building?*

be very careful. What are the dangers? The danger is that a building will warm the ground underneath it and cause the permafrost to melt. The result is that the building will sink or the ground will move and twist the building.

The house shown in Figure 30 is planned for use in the Arctic. For many houses, gravel pads are placed on top of the permafrost. Wood, steel, concrete posts, or jacks which may be adjusted are put on the pads to hold up the building. A space is left between the ground and the floor of the house. This lets the ground stay frozen. And, it may even be colder than it was before as the building will shade the ground from the sun.

For large buildings, wooden or cement posts may be placed deep into the permafrost. Again, the floor of the building is above the ground so that air may flow under it and the permafrost will not melt.

The materials for most buildings in the North must be brought from southern Canada. There

has been much discussion as to how the building should be done. Some people think materials should be brought in and the building constructed on the site. Others think that the building should be built or partly built somewhere else and then erected on the site. This is called a **prefabricated** building. Log wall ways of building have also been used. They are like children's log building sets.

Using the Information

1. List the rooms in the home shown in Figure 29.
2. List the ways in which the house shown is the same as a two-storey house in your community. List how it is different.
3. Where do the materials used to build houses in your community come from?
4. Find out if prefabricated houses are built in your community.

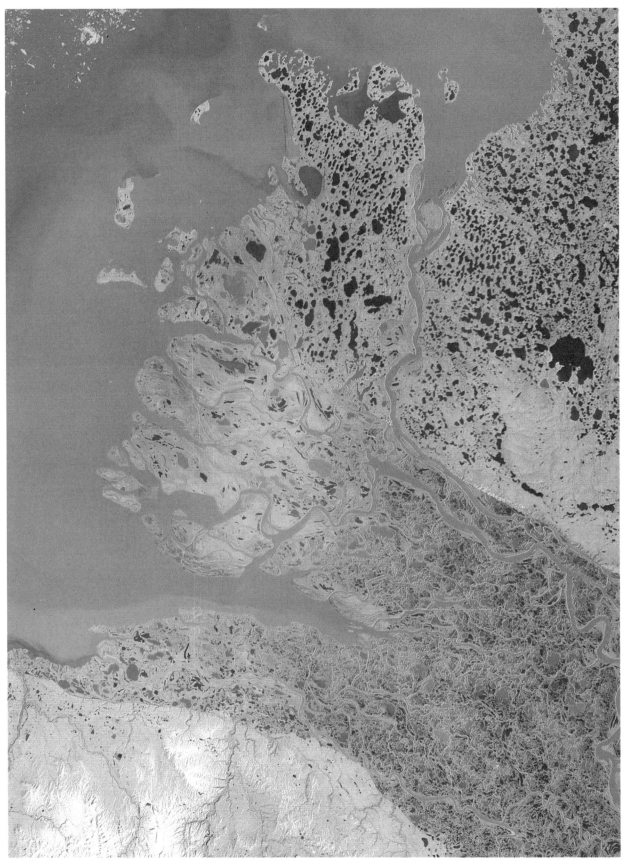

FIGURE 31: How could you describe delta land?

FIGURE 32: Which of the buildings marked on the map below can you find?

Inuvik: A Northern Town

The town of Inuvik is located in the Northwest Territories on the **delta** of the Mackenzie River. It is a new town which was planned for the residents of nearby **Aklavik** and for those people who would come to the area in search of gas and oil. Aklavik was the centre for government, education, and medical help in the western Arctic.

Because it was built on frozen riverland Aklavik has often been flooded in the past. This land could melt and cause problems. The flooding caused health problems and was dangerous to the people living there.

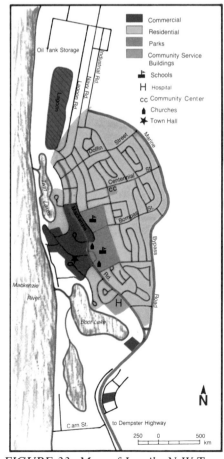

FIGURE 33: Map of Inuvik, N.W.T.

FIGURE 34: Citizens discuss life in a northern community.

The location for Inuvik was chosen because the land is well drained, with good water and air transportation and a good water supply.

Inuvik has grown to about 5000 people. Unfortunately, Aklavik has grown too. Many people have stayed there. Most do not feel they were included when Inuvik was planned. They do not feel it is their town. In fact, some say they first heard about Inuvik on an Alaskan radio station.

Planning a new town can be exciting. It can also be quite difficult in the Arctic. Inuvik is located on permafrost. When the town was built, it was costly and difficult to dig ditches in the permafrost for pipelines to carry water to buildings and away. The solution was to build the pipelines above ground in a structure called a **utilidor**. A utilidor is shown in Figure 35. It is a group of pipes above ground which connect homes. The first utilidor contained four pipes:

1) Carried hot water to heat homes
2) Carried this water away from the homes
3) Carried the water supply, and
4) Carried the sewage

There have been at least eight different kinds of utilidors in Inuvik.

Today things are changing. More powerful **backhoes** and new materials which may be used to insulate pipes has made it possible to bury these pipelines in the permafrost. More and more often this is now being done rather than building utilidors.

Planners must decide what kinds of homes to build in a new community like Inuvik. Inuvik was built to be very much like communities in southern Canada. It was planned so that when people from southern cities came there to stay they would feel quite comfortable.

People coming North have ideas of what a town should be. Most want to see separate houses, duplexes, row houses, and apartments. They want a business section and the town to be planned around buses and roads. Even though the climate and the land around Inuvik is quite different, most expected it to be like

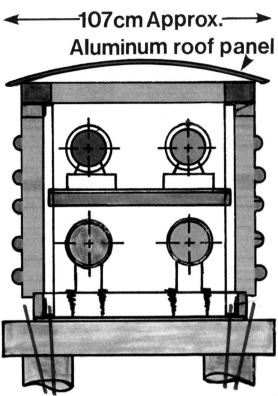

← 107cm Approx. →
Aluminum roof panel

FIGURE 35: What problems does the utilidor cause in a community?

the communities they had left.

Living in a community like Inuvik can be a problem for some people. It is dark 24 hours a day for part of the year and the midnight sun shines from May 26 to July 19. The cold weather often keeps people indoors. This can cause some people to suffer from "cabin fever." When they have cabin fever people often feel sad and lonely.

Read the Map

1. List ways in which the plan of Inuvik is like that of a town in southern Canada.
2. Why is there need for large oil storage tanks?
3. Where are the buildings which many people will use located? Why?
4. Why is the town plan a long rectangle rather than a circle or square?

Using the Information

1. Why was Inuvik built?
2. What problems would a utilidor cause people walking or driving a car in Inuvik?
3. How could this problem be solved?
4. What inventions have made it possible to put pipes underground?
5. Make a sketch of an ideal Arctic home. How will it be built to cut down the wind? For privacy? So that it will not sink into the permafrost? So people will not get "cabin fever?"
6. Draw a plan for a small Arctic town. How will it be different from a town in southern Canada?

Where do people live?

Most people across the North live in small villages and towns on the **Mackenzie Delta**, the Arctic islands, the coast of the Northwest Territories, on the **Quebec** shores of Hudson and **Ungava** bays, and in **Labrador**. These communities are located on bays, river mouths, inlets or fiords, as life in the past was tied to fishing, gathering and hunting.

The number of people in communities may be quite different. In **Kangirsuk**, for example, there are about 260 Inuit and 20 whites. In Frobisher Bay, on the southern tip of Baffin Island, there are about 1400 Inuit and 600 whites.

Kangirsuk, Quebec

Charlie Awa lives in Kangirsuk, Quebec. He tells about his village.

''Kangirsuk is a small village located on the west coast of Ungava Bay. The land is barren. High tides push huge blocks of ice onto the shore in winter. There are no trees.

''Our village has two stores, the Hudson Bay Company and the Co-op. A school, a community hall, a town council, a health clinic, garages and houses are found in our village. We have a **diesel generator** which makes the electricity we use. Our homes use heating oil for fuel. Our water is brought from a lake about 3 km away and is delivered to our homes by a track tractor. Water is stored in small tanks. Sometimes we cut fresh water ice and melt it for water. There are no wells in the village.

''Our clothing is partly handmade and partly store bought. We often still make our winter boots from sealskin. Both parkas and cloth parkas may be seen. Fur parkas made by hand

FIGURE 36: Charlie Awa.

have two layers. The outer layer of skin has the fur side facing out. The inner layers have the fur side facing in. Fox fur is often used to trim parkas and jackets. We wear store bought trousers, shirts, dresses, slacks, and undergarments. We buy our clothes from the two stores in town.

"Each August a supply ship brings goods such as food, clothing, kitchen appliances, new houses, snowmobiles, vehicles, and oil. Airplanes bring mail, people, and smaller goods into the village two or three times each week.

"We obtain a great deal of our food ourselves. We hunt caribou, seal, ptarmigan, and geese. There is always a good supply of fish, including Arctic Char.

"Caribou are important to our village. These animals are not raised like beef cattle in southern Canada. They must be hunted as they move around the barrens. There is too little food for them to be kept in one place for very long.

"There are just under 300 people in our village. Besides hunting and fishing there are many other jobs in the village. They include:

FIGURE 37

FIGURE 38

Prepare a sketch map of Kangirsuk.

FIGURE 39

97

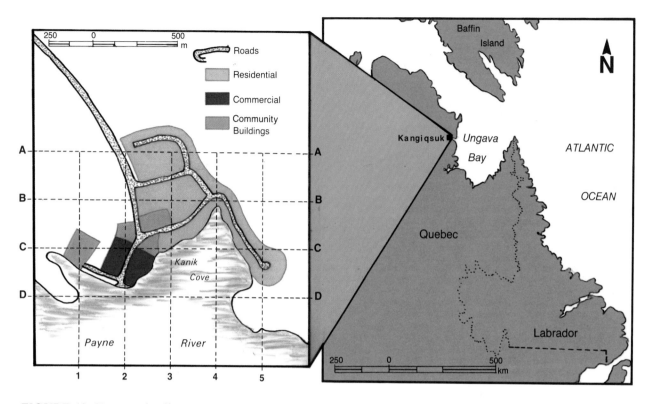

FIGURE 41: Kangirsuk village.

Co-op manager
air agent
five teachers
welfare worker
nursing assistant
two repairmen
two mechanic helpers
craftworkers

Co-op assistants
Hudson Bay manager
three janitors
two nurses
policeman
a mechanic
four water, fuel, and
garbage tractor drivers

"There are only a few white people in our village. Most are Inuit like me. Many of the villagers only speak our language, Inuttitut."

Using the Information

1. In the past villagers needed little money to live. Why do they need money today?
2. Why are caribou hunted?
3. Why are there few cars and trucks in Kangirsuk?
4. There are many snowmobiles and outboard motors in Kangirsuk. Why?
5. Why was Kangirsuk located on the shore of Ungava Bay?

Read the Map

1. Sketch symbols that might be used on the map for houses, church, store, or airport.
2. What direction is the town from Ungava Bay?

FIGURE 42: What dangers must a barge captain avoid?

How are goods and people transported?

Transportation is extremely important to northern communities. These communities need good links with communities in southern Canada. These links are made in a number of ways.

Each summer, many northern communities are visited by supply ships and barges. From July to early October machinery, tools, food, and other bulk supplies are carried into the Arctic.

The **Mackenzie River** is used as a main waterway to bring loads from southern Canada. The boats and barges bring machinery for mines and oil wells, prefabricated buildings, lumber equipment for buildings, and homes.

In 1984 the first Arctic trip was made by a passenger ship. The name of the ship was the **M/S Lindblad Explorer** (M/S stands for

motor ship). It sailed from **St. John's, Newfoundland** to the **Chukchi Sea** on the way to Japan.

FIGURE 43: Journey of the cruise ship Lindblad Explorer.

99

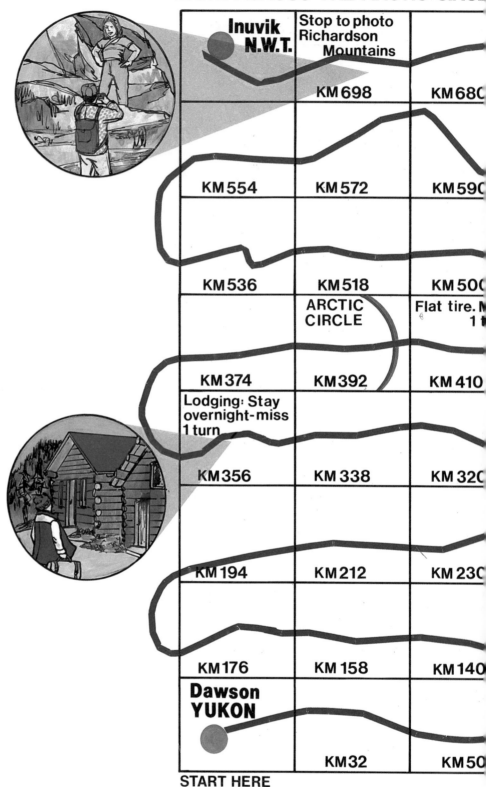

Inuvik N.W.T.	Stop to photo Richardson Mountains	
KM 698		KM 680
KM 554	KM 572	KM 590
KM 536	KM 518	KM 500
	ARCTIC CIRCLE	Flat tire. M... 1 t
KM 374	KM 392	KM 410
Lodging: Stay overnight-miss 1 turn		
KM 356	KM 338	KM 320
KM 194	KM 212	KM 230
KM 176	KM 158	KM 140
Dawson YUKON		
	KM 32	KM 50

START HERE

Dempster Highway Game

KM 662	KM 644
KM 608	KM 626
NORTHWEST TERRITORIES	**YUKON**
KM 482	KM 464
KM 428	KM 446
KM 302	KM 284
owstorm. Go ck 2 spaces	
KM 248	KM 266
apman Lake. ss 1 turn and view	Blackstone River. Miss 1 turn and go fishing
KM 122	KM 104
	Road crosses the North Klondike River
KM 68	KM 86

FIGURE 44: THE DEMPSTER HIGHWAY GAME DIRECTIONS:
1. You will need a die and marker.
2. Play with a classmate.
3. Place your marker(s) on the Dawson, Yukon square.
4. Take turns throwing the die.
5. The winner is the player who arrives at Inuvik, N.W.T., first.
6. Have a good trip!

101

FIGURE 45: *Unloading cargo from an airplane to a snowmobile.*

Aircraft

Airplanes have changed the North. For many communities the airstrip has become the main street of their town. Air service now means that northerners may be transported to hospitals within hours of an accident. Large cargo planes bring in even some of the bulky supplies needed.

Small airplanes are used to move people and goods between settlements. And, helicopters have proven very useful in transporting goods to places where landing airplanes might be difficult.

Frequent fogs and long periods of darkness can cause airflight delays in some parts of the North.

Ground Transportation

As we have already seen, the snowmobile has changed ground transportation. Within communities and between communities, the buzz of a snowmobile engine is a common sound.

Larger snowmobiles and track vehicles are used to carry larger loads. Unloading planes and ships requires the use of trucks. In many communities there is little need for a car.

Read the Map

1. List the islands and communities the M/S Lindblad Explorer passed.
2. List the bodies of water the M/S Lindblad Explorer sailed.

Use the Information

1. Make sketches in your notebook of three ways of travelling in the North.
2. Give a reason why railways are not built in the North.
3. The North has small communities with long distances between them. What transportation problems does this cause?

A Problem To Ponder

A National Park on Ellesmere Island:

Do We Need One?

Ellesmere Island is the most northern part of our country. The town of Alert is our most northerly settlement on the island. The North Pole is only 600 km away!

The government made a plan to make a northern part of the island a wilderness park. Backpacking, hiking, cross-country skiing and nature study are some of the activities which would be allowed in the park.

Read the following fact sheet about the area. Then read the arguments and see what you think.

Landscape:

Three different kinds of landscape

a) The **Grant Land Mountains**
Barbeau Peak, 2616 metres, is the highest. Mountains are covered with ice up to 1900 metres thick.

b) **Hazen Plateau**
A large plateau area with Hazen Lake located on it.

c) A coast with many fiords

Wildlife

small herd of musk oxen
Peary caribou
arctic wolf
arctic hare
arctic fox
seals
lemmings
long tailed jaegers
arctic terns
snow geese
snow buntings
snow owls
loons
king eider ducks
120 kinds of plants and 160 kinds of mosses.

History

Artifacts from the Inuit over 4,000 years old.

Cairns which mark the visit of British explorer **Sir George Nares**.

Fort Conger where **Greely** built a large house in 1881.

House was dismantled by the Arctic explorer **Peary** who built three smaller buildings. Remains of these huts may be seen today.

FIGURE 46: Caribou, Northwest Territories.

103

FIGURE 47: Do we need a national park on Ellesmere Island?

NO

This part of Ellesmere Island is very fragile. Now it is made a park visitors will come. They will destroy the plant and animal life forever.

YES

The park is so far north there will be few visitors to destroy the environment.

NO

Foot trails and vehicle tracks made 30 years ago may still be seen today. We know very little about how long it takes the environment to recover from damage that we do to it.

YES

Now it is made into a park the area will be protected for people in the future. There will be park rangers there to make sure the environment is not hurt.

NO

The remains of Peary and his expedition are still there today. Tourists will destroy this early history of our country.

YES

If they are left out in the open these remains will be destroyed anyway. Those remains belong in a museum.

Unit 5

Onto A Shield of Rock

What is the Canadian Shield?

The Canadian Shield is the name given to a large area of land around Hudson Bay. Geographers have given it this name. Even the shape is like that of a shield. Although almost half of Canada's land is in this region, few people live there.

FIGURE 1

FIGURE 2

FIGURE 3

Write a caption for each photograph.

FIGURE 4

FIGURE 5

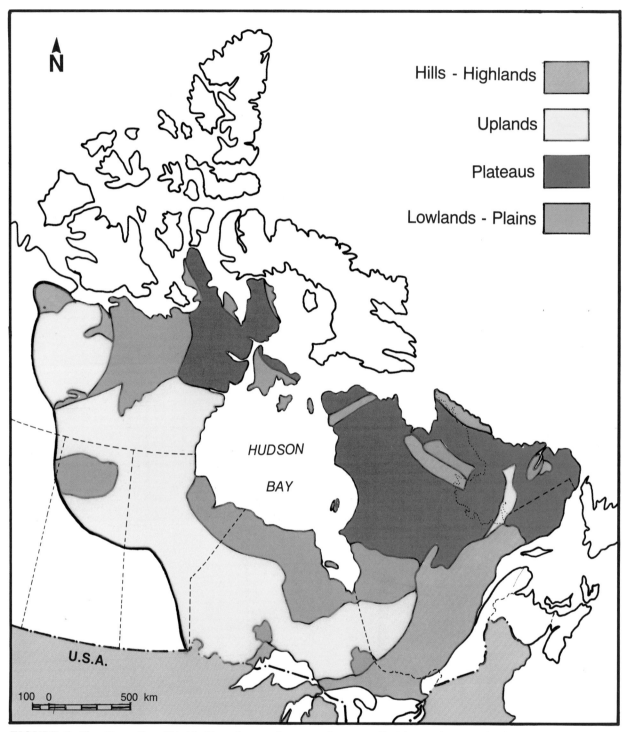

FIGURE 6: The Canadian Shield. Do other regions you have studied have shapes which you recognize?

The sketches below show how scientists think the Canadian Shield was formed.

Using the Information

1. How did the Canadian Shield get its name?
2. Correct this generalization: "Much of the Canadian population lives on the Canadian Shield."
3. Why do scientists not know definitely how the shield was formed?

FIGURE 7: Scientists believe that thousands of years ago this part of Canada was mountainous.

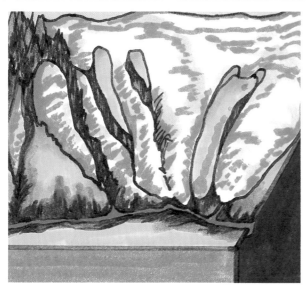

FIGURE 8: Sheets of ice called glaciers moved south. They ground down the tops of the mountains.

FIGURE 9: They scraped off much of the top soil. The ice scooped out valleys and moved tonnes of rocks.

FIGURE 10: When the ice melted it left great loads of earth and rock. Rivers were dammed. Gravel was dropped.

FIGURE 11: The work of glaciers uncovered valuable minerals like iron and gold.

What is the climate like on the Canadian Shield?

The Canadian Shield covers a large part of Canada. It borders the Arctic Ocean in the north. It includes **Lake Superior** in the south. It stretches from Alberta to Newfoundland. In such a large space there are many differences in climate. The charts and photographs show information for five places on the shield.

The crops and plants which may be grown in places on the shield depend on more than the length of the growing season. For

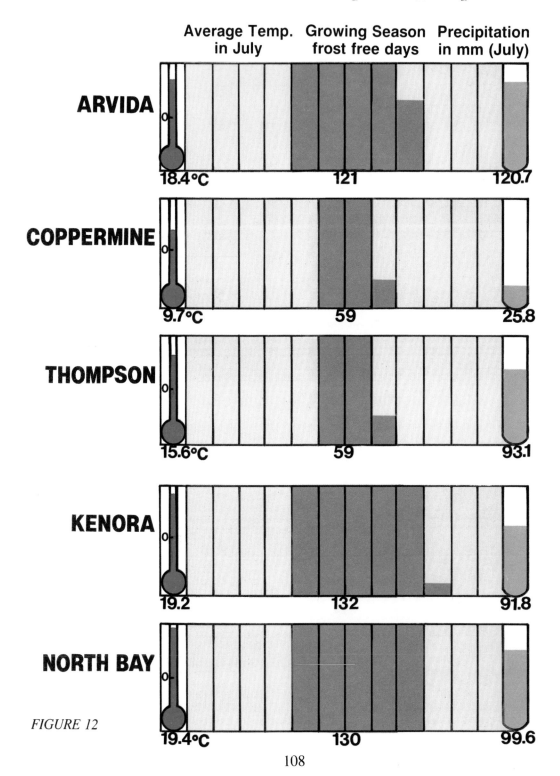

	Average Temp. in July	Growing Season frost free days	Precipitation in mm (July)
ARVIDA	18.4°C	121	120.7
COPPERMINE	9.7°C	59	25.8
THOMPSON	15.6°C	59	93.1
KENORA	19.2	132	91.8
NORTH BAY	19.4°C	130	99.6

FIGURE 12

108

FIGURE 13: *North Bay.*

FIGURE 14: *Arvida.*

FIGURE 15: *Coppermine.*

FIGURE 16: *Thompson.*

example, if fields are in a valley, the sun may be trapped and cause high daytime temperatures. In some northern settlements the

Read the Charts

1. Use your atlas to locate each town.
2. How are the temperatures in the five locations the same? Different?
3. How is the precipitation in the five locations the same? Different?

long hours of summer daylight make up for the short growing season. There, crops grow faster.

4. How is the growing season in the five locations the same? Different?
5. Write a sentence telling about:
   a) winter in each location
   b) summer in each location
6. Write a generalization about the climate on the Canadian Shield.

What resources are found on the Canadian Shield?

Nearly one of every eight Canadians have chosen to live on the Canadian Shield. Some people have jobs in the mines and on power projects. Others earn their living by hunting and trapping. The forestry industry employs a number of people.

Some people, who live in large towns, help workers by supplying the goods and services they need.

The Canadian Shield has many resources that are needed by Canadians who live in other parts of the country. One valuable resource is the fast-flowing rivers. They can be used to make electricity. Most Canadians rely on electricity to heat and light their homes.

Read the Diagram

What is the number of each of the following:
A. Carries electricity to cities.
B. Holds back the water.
C. Keeps rocks from falling into the turbine.
D. A motor turned by the water.
E. Carries the water to the turbine.

FIGURE 17: A hydro-electric power station.

The James Bay Project

Henri Letendre is an engineer. He works in the control room of a hydro-electric power station. The station is the **La Grande River** power station in northern Quebec.

Henri's job is to watch how the station is working. By reading meters and gauges, Henri is able to tell what is happening.

The sketch shows how electricity is made from water. Although the idea is fairly simple, the equipment and machines used are quite complicated. It takes well-trained people like Henri to keep the station working.

In 1971 the government of Quebec started the **James Bay Project**. It was a large project planned to use rivers to make electricity.

The La Grande River flows into **James Bay**. It was dammed. A power station was built. The electricity is sold to people who live in and around the city of Montréal. It is also sold to customers in the United States.

The James Bay Project has changed the landscape. A dam was built across the La Grande River. When the dam was completed, a lake began to fill behind it. This huge **reservoir** covered land, bush, and trees. Beneath the water valuable trap-lines disappeared.

FIGURE 18: *Inside a power station.*

FIGURE 19: *Henri Letendre.*

111

An Issue to Ponder

Should northern rivers be dammed to make electricity?

The building of the James Bay Project was not welcomed by all people. Some were worried about the environment. The Native peoples, who lived on the land where the project was built, were concerned.

NO

The flooding changes many things. Timber, wild rice fields, Indian reserves, and small animal homes are lost. Where trappers used to get many muskrat, these animals are now hard to find. Fishing is ruined because of sticks and other floating objects.

If the land is flooded it will destroy the past of the Indian people. We worry about the graves of our ancestors. They are covered when the land is flooded. It hurts our people when these links with the past are lost.

YES

A great deal of money has been spent studying these projects. Other projects have also been studied. We know enough now to build the dams without hurting the environment.

These projects help bring Native people a new way of life. They will learn new jobs. They will be able to live like people in southern Canada.

FIGURE 20: Edna Redgrave, Chuck Birchill, Eli Bigblood, and Chief Wilson Noonias discuss the James Bay Project.

112

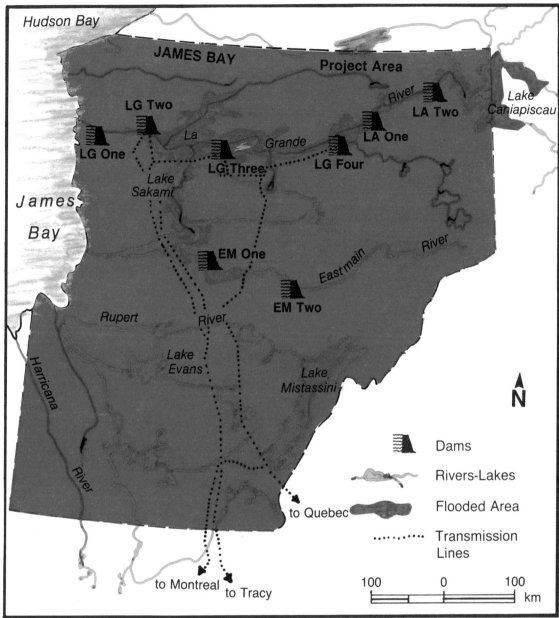

FIGURE 21: Where are dams built?

Using the Information

1. What is the James Bay Project?
2. Where are hydro stations located? Why?
3. Why are hydro-electric stations needed?
4. How do dam sites change the landscape?
5. Where does the electrical power for your home come from?
6. How would you feel if a dam caused land owned by your family to be flooded?

In The Forest

How is wood used in your community? What things are made of wood in your home? Where does that wood come from? Many of the people who live on the Canadian Shield work in forest **industries.** Eric Cardinal of **Geraldton,** Ontario, is one of these people.

A Forest Worker

The Cardinal family have lived in Geraldton for many years. The two boys in the family, Rob and Randy, go to high school there. Their mother, Mary, works in a bank. Eric, their father, works in the forest.

Unlike the rest of the family, Eric spends most of the week away from town. Each Sunday afternoon he leaves his home and drives to a logging camp. He stays and works at this camp all week. On Friday he drives home.

Eric's camp is made up of trailers. These trailers can be moved from place to place in the forest. Eric Cardinal shares a room with Jorn. Jorn is also a lumberjack.

The men in the camp have their meals in a large dining room. In their spare time they often go to the recreation room. There they play table tennis, snooker, or watch television. Sometimes they just sit around and talk with other workers.

FIGURE 22: Eric's camp.

FIGURE 23: The Cardinal Family.

114

FIGURE 24: Which of these trees grow in or near your community?

Each day a truck takes Eric to the place where trees are being cut. Eric cuts **balsam fir** and black **spruce** trees. These grow together in this part of Ontario. **Conifers,** such as fir and spruce trees, grow well here. They have roots that spread out near the surface and are able to grow in the short growing season.

Eric uses a chain saw to cut the trees into logs. These logs are then loaded onto large trucks. The trucks transport them to a paper mill. The diagram shows what happens to the logs as they move from the forest to market.

FIGURE 25: From forest to newsprint.

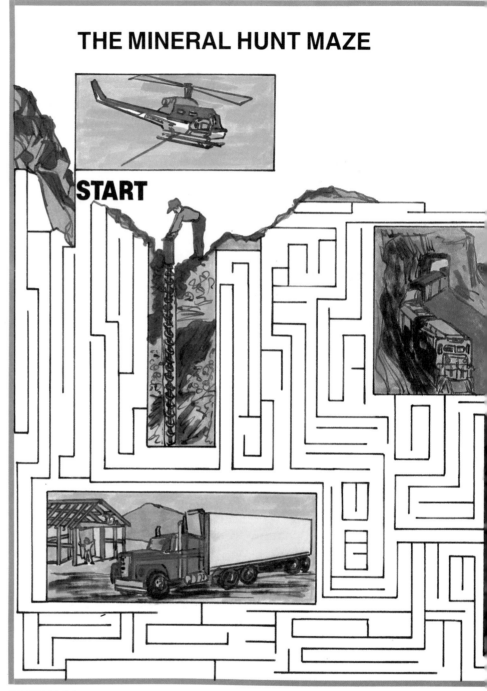

THE MINERAL HUNT MAZE

START

FIGURE 26

Mineral Hunt Maze

Many of the things we use every day depend upon the minerals taken from the earth. Follow the maze and see some of the steps taken to bring some of those products to you.

Please do not write on the maze.
1. Aircraft use instruments to find minerals.
2. Holes are drilled to find minerals and tell how big the find might be.

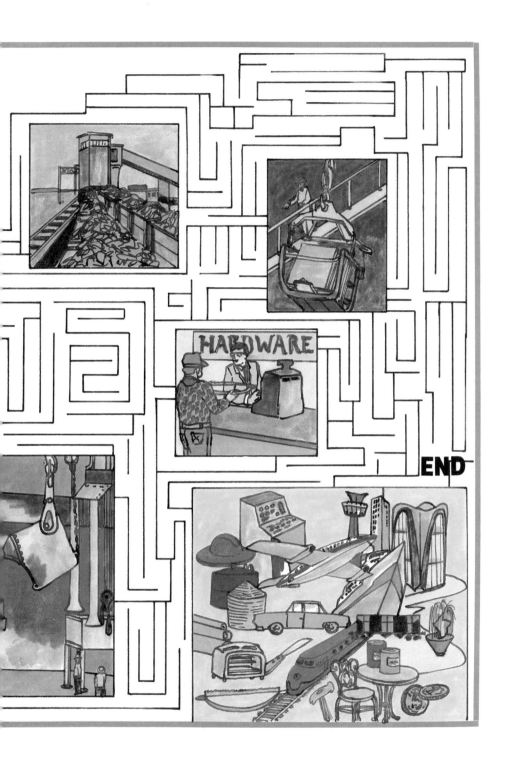

3. Equipment and supplies are brought in to start a town.
4. A railroad is built to take the mineral to a plant.
5. Ore from the mine is made into metal.

6. The metal is sent to factories in Canada and around the world.
7. Factories use the metal to make products.
8. Products are sold to people in stores.
9. How many things made from metal can you find in this picture?

FIGURE 27: A slice of life in an early lumber camp.

The forest industry hires many Canadians such as Eric to cut trees. Many others are kept busy in mills making paper. Newsprint, paperboard, and building materials are all made from trees.

More than half of the newspapers printed in North America are printed on newsprint from Canada. Out of every 100 box cars of newsprint:

    8 stay in Canada

   15 go to countries overseas

   77 are sold to the United States

Read the Diagram

1. Make symbols for the diagram on page 115, to show what happens as trees are turned into paper.

Using the Information

1. The painting shows life in a lumber camp in the past. List the ways life for Eric might be different from life for these lumberjacks.

FIGURE 28: Machines help forest workers.

FIGURE 29: A central place.

Where do people live?

Where does your family shop for groceries, furniture, clothing, or sports equipment? Why have those stores been built in those locations? Most stores are built near the centre of communities for two reasons:

1. The centre is the shortest travelling distance from most homes, and
2. once at the centre it is a short distance to other stores and businesses.

The locations where these stores are built are called central places. Large communities may have many central places.

Whole villages, towns, and cities may also be central places. They are the centre for people in the surrounding area. There are different kinds of central places on the Canadian Shield.

Indian and Inuit settlements were some of the first central places on the shield. When people from Europe arrived they built fur trading forts which were also central places.

Today most of the central places are small settlements, towns, or small cities. Many of these places have grown because of resources which are found nearby. **Thompson,** Manitoba, is an example of a central place which grew very quickly.

Thompson, Manitoba: A Mining City

Thompson is one of the largest central places on the shield. It grew to be a city in a

FIGURE 30: Thompson, Manitoba, in the 1950s.

very short time. It was settled so that nickel, found in the rock nearby, could be mined.

Prospectors had been looking for minerals in northern Manitoba for years. Old rotted **claim stakes** from the 1920s and 1930s prove this.

Finally a company called **Inco Metals** found a large amount of nickel. There was enough **ore** to start a mine.

The ore was far away from the closest settlements so the company decided to build a new town. Where should the school be built? What about a hospital? A plan was drawn. Every road

FIGURE 31: How has Thompson changed?

and public building had to be planned.

Inco Metals wanted to begin mining as soon as possible. The nearest railroad was over 45 kilometres to the south. To transport supplies from the railway to the new mine and town, the Snowball Express was started.

The Snowball Express was a diesel-powered tractor train. The trains crossed over the frozen lakes and **muskeg** to carry materials to the mine and town. Each train had two crews. One crew slept and ate while the other worked. As the town was built, so was a railway. Soon the Snowball Express was no longer needed.

Construction camps were built for the workers. A hospital, water and sewer lines, schools, churches, and stores were built. In five years, the new town opened. It was named after Dr. John Thompson. Dr. Thompson had worked for Inco Metals for many years.

By 1970 Thompson had grown large enough to be known as a city. Thompson has grown as a central place for many reasons. First, there was a need for people to work in the mine. Then, when these people arrived, they needed goods and services. Look at the chart shown below. Would you find these businesses in your community?

The large smokestack in Thompson is a sign of a problem. In changing ore to nickel, **wastes** are let off into the air. These wastes pass into the air through the huge smokestack.

FIGURE 32: Thompson businesses.

121

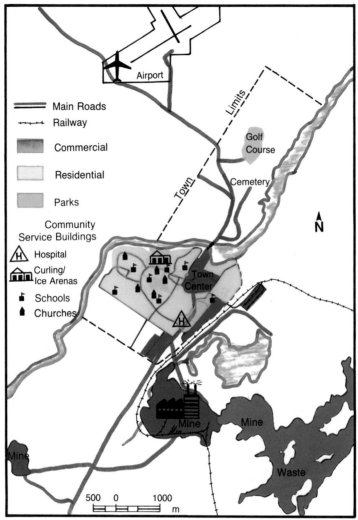

FIGURE 33: Thompson, Manitoba.

In and around Thompson, the air, water, and growing plants are watched. The direction of the wind and air temperature are watched too. If too much waste is going into the air, the plant must slow down. Keeping the environment clean is a special problem for this city.

Read the Map

1. Many young families moved to Thompson. What facilities on the town plan are for young people?
2. Where are the businesses located in Thompson? Why?
3. Where are the homes located? Why?
4. Why is the mine located where it is? Think about the wind direction when you answer this question.

Using the Information

1. What is a central place?
2. What is the name of the central place in which you live?
3. Why was the city of Thompson started?
4. Why did the town grow?
5. Use your atlas and make a list of ten other central places found on the Canadian Shield.
6. What might happen if the nickel ore near Thompson was all mined?
7. If there is possible danger to the environment, why does mining at Thompson continue?

How do people earn a living on the Canadian Shield?

Henri Letendre and the Cardinal family earn their living in jobs connected with two important natural resources found on the Canadian Shield. The Whitfield family and the McNays do quite different kinds of work.

Susan and Joe Whitfield: Trappers

In September Susan and Joe Whitfield leave **Yellowknife, Northwest Territories**. They fly to **Watta Lake** where they trap each year. They have built a six metre by six metre cabin.

The Whitfields take a supply of food with them. These foods do not need to be

FIGURE 34: The Whitfields.

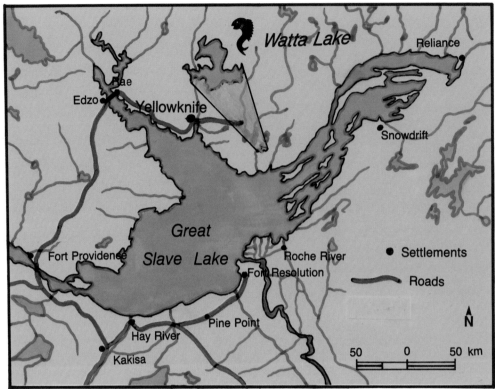

FIGURE 35: The Watta Lake area.

refrigerated. They take no meat. Instead, they catch fish or hunt birds such as **ptarmigan.** Moose and bear are also hunted. By mid-October the temperature is cold enough for meat to be hung outside to freeze.

Once they have enough meat for the winter, they begin catching and storing fish for their dogs. Although most trappers own snow-mobiles, many still like to use dog teams. Dogs don't break down and leave a trapper stranded miles from camp.

Trappers drive between four and nine dogs. Often they cover up to 80 kilometres each day checking traplines. This is hard on the dogs, so spares are needed. Travelling in the deep snow is hard work. It is little wonder that a dog may eat two pounds of fish a day.

Fox, mink, lynx, marten, weasel, wolf, muskrat, beaver, and wolverine are trapped. The best fur is caught in mid-December when there are only four or five hours of daylight. Often the temperatures are -30° C to -40° C.

The fur is hard to get. Animals do not move around much in the cold. Trappers may spend a lot of time in the cold and get very few animals.

Bait thieves, such as ravens and jays, may cause problems. They steal the bait from the traps.

Furs are sold in town or sent to southern Canadian cities to be auctioned. The furs will bring a higher price at the auction. However, it will be two or three months before the trapper gets paid.

By mid-March the trapping season is over for all animals except beaver and muskrat. Trappers move back to town ready to celebrate with their friends. Winter carnivals with dancing, games, and dog races are held in many northern communities.

Most trappers do not make a lot of money. Their way of life is more important to them. Many are living much like their ancestors did in the North.

Should people trap animals for fur? Some Canadians say "NO!" They believe it is cruel to kill animals for clothing. They ask "Would you kill a family pet for a new pair of fur mitts?"

Read the Map

1. What direction from Yellowknife is Watta Lake?
2. Why do the Whitfields use an airplane to reach their camp?
3. Where are the settlements around Yellowknife located? Why?
4. Name the settlements on **Great Slave Lake.**

Using the Information

1. Why do the Whitfields not take meat with them to their camp?
2. What is done with the furs which are trapped?
3. What is important to the Whitfields when they choose a job?
4. List three questions you would ask the Whitfields about the life of a trapper.
5. If the temperature in the North increased, what might happen?

FIGURE 36: The Whitfields' cabin.

The McNays: Resort Owners

The beautiful lakes and rivers of northern Ontario are the perfect setting for the McNays' hunting and fishing lodge. Molly McNay and her husband, Terry, run the lodge deep in the Canadian wilderness. While Molly manages the resort, her husband handles the guests' fishing and hunting needs.

The lodge is about 150 kilometres north of **Kenora,** Ontario. It is located on the edge of a lake. Twenty guest log cottages have been built along the shore. These cottages have modern washrooms with showers and hot water. They are heated by electric heaters.

The main lodge has a large dining room where home-cooked meals are served to guests. A crackling fire in the huge stone fireplace welcomes guests to the lounge each evening. There they relax or trade fish stories.

Managing the lodge, which has as many as one hundred guests at a time, is a big job. Guests come from all over Canada and the United States to hunt deer, bear, and moose. Lake trout, walleye, and bass are plentiful for fishermen.

FIGURE 37: The McNays.

FIGURE 38: The McNays' resort.

126

Molly and Terry feel they are lucky to be located in the North. Molly has always wanted to run her own business. Terry has always loved the outdoors. Their resort allows them both to do what they want. It also provides them with a good living.

The McNays are part of the tourist industry. Providing for tourists is an important activity in many parts of the Canadian Shield. For example, it is the third largest industry after forestry and mining in northern Ontario.

A look at Kenora, Ontario, shows how important tourists can be. Tourism there helps keep the following businesses operating:

521 hotel rooms

21 gas stations

38 restaurants

7 china and gift shops

8 souvenir shops

9 sports, bait, and tackle shops

4 airlines

FIGURE 39: Kenora businesses.

Using the Information

1. Why is the McNays' resort located in the forest?
2. What jobs must be done at the resort?
3. What services do tourists need?
4. Why do the McNays run a resort? What was important to them in choosing a job?
5. Write an advertisement to attract people to the McNays' resort.
6. Suppose your advertisement works. Many people want to come to the resort. What do you think might happen?

Maps to Make

1. Prepare a sketch map of the Whitfields' camp on Watta Lake.
   a) Draw the shoreline of the lake along one edge of your paper.
   b) Sketch the outline of the cabin.
   c) Show where the trees are located.
   d) Sketch a pier for boats and airplanes.
   e) Make a legend for your map.
2. Sketch a map of the McNays' resort.
   a) Sketch the shore of the lake along one edge of your paper.
   b) Sketch the main lodge and the log cottages.
   c) Sketch in the paths between the log cottages.
   c) Sketch in the road to the cottages.
   d) Draw in the pier.
   e) Sketch in the garage/workshop.
   f) Show where the trees are located.

FIGURE 40: The Benton family.

The Bentons: A Mining Family

Sam Benton is a miner. This month Sam works on the evening shift. When most of us are thinking of going to bed, Sam is beginning to work.

Sam drives to work in his car. When he arrives he puts on special clothes for his job. Each worker has a locker. Sam keeps his working clothes in it. He wears a safety hat with a lamp. Because it may get wet in the mine he wears rubber pants, coat, and boots. To protect his eyes from pieces of flying rock, he wears safety glasses.

As soon as he is ready he gets into the cage. The cage is an elevator that lowers people into the mine shaft. Sam gets off when the cage stops at his level.

He walks along the level to the place where he and his partners work. Holes are drilled into the rock. Explosives are put into the holes.

FIGURE 41: How do these clothes protect miners?

128

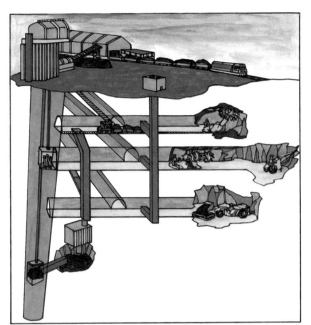

FIGURE 42: Cross-section of an underground mine.

The rock that is blasted out is put into cars with a loader. These cars on rails take the rock to the mine shaft where it is lifted to the surface.

Part way through the shift Sam and his partner will stop for lunch. Lunch is eaten in an underground room. When their shift is finished the cage lifts them to the surface. After a shower and a change of clothes Sam returns home.

Laureen and Sam Benton live with their three children. The home which they rent from the mining company is close to schools and a shopping center. The Benton children all go to nearby schools.

The family takes part in many community activities. Sam is a hockey and baseball coach. Laureen is president of the community association. All three Benton children play a number of different sports.

As active as they are in the community, the Bentons will someday move away. They want the children to have a good education. They know the children will have to leave this mining community if they are to go to college or a technical school.

Laureen and Sam have plans for their own future too. Sam earns good money for the work he does. They save some of this money each month.

They are looking forward to the day when they will have saved enough money to move back to **Toronto**. They would like to start a small business there.

Read the Diagram

1. Draw a symbol which could be used to show each part of the mine.
2. Why are there **stopes** which are not in the ore-bearing rock?
3. Sketch the mine in your notebooks. Draw arrows to show the route which the ore follows from stope to mill.

Using the Information

.1 What special clothing does Sam Benton wear? Why?
2. Why is lunch eaten underground instead of at home or on the surface?
3. What problems do miners and their families face?
4. What reasons might families like the Bentons have for going and working in a northern mining town?

How are people and goods transported on the Canadian Shield?

Many communities on the shield are not joined by highways or railways. Moving people and loads has been a problem. There has been a change from the use of waterways to the use of railways, highways, and airways. However, the distances between settlements, the landscape, high costs, and the weather still make transportation difficult in some places.

Over Water

How to get traders into parts of the north and how to get furs out was an early transportation problem. The solution was to use birch bark canoes.

Birch bark canoes were very useful. They could carry up to two tonnes of furs. They were light and could be carried around waterfalls and over **portages.**

Furs were carried out of parts of the north in large canoes until about 1800. At that time there was a new boat built in the settlement at **York Factory.** It was called the York boat.

York boats were used for many reasons. They were stronger than canoes. They could carry large loads and they needed fewer crew members than canoes did.

York boats were about three metres by 12 metres. This is a little less than half the size of a classroom. An advantage of these boats was the many ways in which they could be powered. If there was a wind, a square sail could be used. In

FIGURE 43: How is this truck equipped to travel over rough land?

130

FIGURE 44: A large cargo plane in the 1930s, ready to be loaded.

shallow water the boats were pushed with poles. They could be rowed, hauled with ropes by crews on shore over rapids, and even rolled over portages.

Over Land

The rock base on the shield presented problems for railway builders. Rock had to be moved so that a level rail bed could be built. Hills had to be levelled and the water level of some lakes lowered to make way for the track.

Factories had to be built to make the dynamite needed to blast away the rock. Working with dynamite was dangerous. In building one piece of the railway, more than 30 people were killed. Explosions and falling rocks took their lives.

Muskeg, which is a thick layer of moss and plants soaked with water, caused problems too.

Tonnes of gravel and rock were dumped into these spongy lakes to make the rail bed. Much of the gravel sank away into the muskeg. Tracks, and even locomotives, sank out of sight.

As if these problems were not enough, workers on the railway faced insects and mosquitoes which bit them day and night.

Railways are a good way of transporting large bulky loads. Since the first railway was built, many more have been constructed. They move heavy loads such as minerals and lumber across the shield.

In the Air

The coming of the airplane opened many new parts of the shield. For some communities today the airplane is the only transportation link with other communities.

131

Most communities have some kind of air service.

Interesting stories are told about the first pilots who flew into parts of the shield. These "bush pilots," as they were called, were people like Orville J. Wieben.

Orville Wieben: Bush Pilot

Orville Wieben was born on a wheat farm in Saskatchewan. He wanted to learn to fly. To earn money for flying lessons, Orville worked as a farm labourer and fed hogs and cattle.

During the Second World War, Orville was a flying instructor and a test pilot. He was one of the first Canadians to learn to fly by instruments.

Orville started his own airline. At first, he flew **pulpwood** cutters into bush camps. Soon he had a fleet of 30 aircraft.

Orville became famous in Canada for his "Santa Claus" flights. Each Christmas he flew gifts of clothing and toys to remote Native settlements. He also made **"mercy"** flights to help people who were sick or injured. He helped search for people and planes lost in the northern bush.

He had spent over 30,000 hours in the air when he died in 1979.

Using the Information

1. List the ways people travel and move goods on the shield.
2. What problems are there in travelling on some parts of the shield?
3. What is a bush pilot?
4. What is the best way to move large bulky loads? Why?
5. If more highways were built in northern parts of the shield, what might happen?
6. If more people moved to settlements on the northern parts of the shield, what might happen?

What ideas and inventions have helped people on the Canadian Shield?

The land, the climate, and the long distances between places have created problems for people on the shield. To solve some of these problems, Canadians have borrowed ideas from others. For other problems we have had to find our own solutions. As you read about some of these ideas and inventions, think how they have changed the landscape of the Canadian Shield.

From Snowmobiles to Satellites

Providing transportaiton on the shield has led to the use of some unusual inventions.

Snowmobiles are widely used on the shield. These vehicles need no road. They travel at speeds up to 95 km/h. They carry loads up to 1300 kg. Many people own a snowmobile much as southern Canadians own a car.

Snowmobiles are very reliable. However, should there be a breakdown, most owners have become expert at making their own repairs.

The lack of roads has led to a number of other inventions.

The Aerobec has been invented to travel over muskeg, water, and cleared land. An off-road vehicle that works partly like a hovercraft and partly like a track vehicle, it is being built by two companions in Montréal. It will carry heavy loads.

The Aerobec will be able to carry a seven-tonne load and up to 30 people. It will travel over rough trails and muskeg at 30 km/h.

Mobile homes have made it possible for people in many settlements on the shield to have modern and comfortable homes.

Moving materials and tradesmen to many of these communities to build homes would not be possible. The mobile homes are built in southern Canada. They are built in different sizes and shapes. They can be moved into communities by truck, train, and even by air.

Earth satellites have helped solve the problem of loneliness for some people. Television by satellite can provide even the most faraway communities with a choice of channels from around the world.

In addition, radio and two-way radios have helped people on the shield keep in touch with each other.

Using the Information

1. List the ways you hear about a new toy or piece of sports equipment.
2. List the ways Canadians learn about new inventions used in other parts of the world. How is this list the same as the items in Question #1? Different?
3. Cold winters still cause problems for many shield communities. List some ideas or inventions that might make life easier.

FIGURE 45: A satellite communications tower.

Unit 6
Next to the Great Lakes

What are the land and water like in the Great Lakes region?

Scientists believe that the land where the Great Lakes are now located was once covered with very deep sheets of ice. As this ice moved, melted, and refroze, it shaped the land beneath it. Valleys were dug, hollows were scoured out and hills were formed. The marks of this shaping may be seen on the land today. When this ice sheet finally melted it left behind what we call the Great Lakes.

In the past the Great Lakes were much larger than they are today. At one time they were drained by many rivers. Today the levels have dropped. The lakes are smaller and they

FIGURE 1

FIGURE 2

List the things you see in photograhs 1, 2, 3 and 4. Group those items which seem to belong together. Write a sentence about each of these groups, which tells about the landscape next to the Great Lakes.

FIGURE 3

FIGURE 4

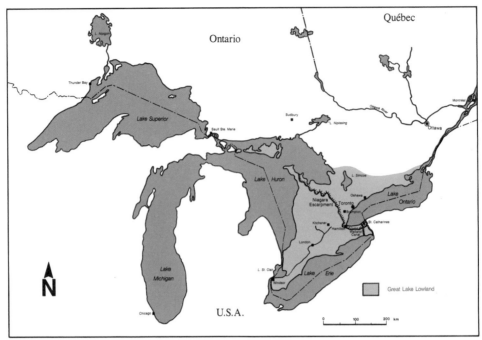

FIGURE 5: *The Great Lakes Lowland.*

are drained by only one river, the St. Lawrence.

The land shown in Figure 5 is known as the **Great Lakes Lowland**. It was covered with dust, sand, gravel, rocks, and mud left behind as the ice melted. The land is made up of plains, hills, and **escarpments.** The most important of these is the **Niagara Escarpment.**

The sketch in Figure 6 shows an escarpment or scarp. It is formed by the wearing away of rocks. Some rocks are weak and wear away easily. Others are hard and do not wear so quickly. When a river flows over these two kinds of rock, it wears away the weak rock faster. Soon a

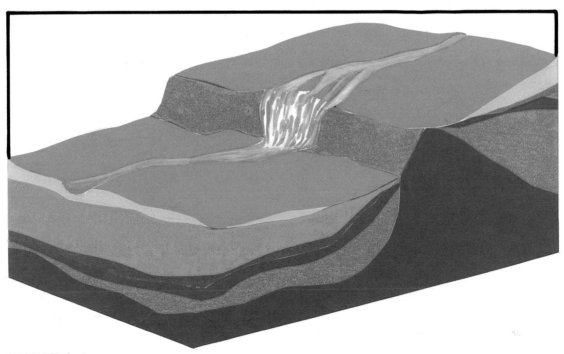

FIGURE 6: *An escarpment.*

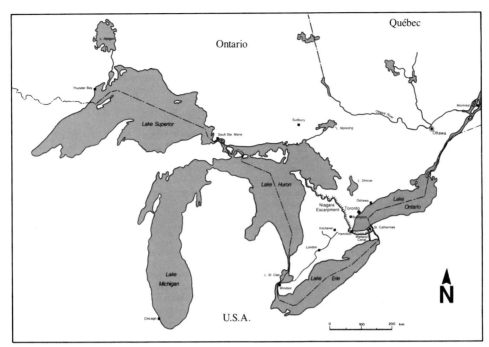

FIGURE 7: Map of the Great Lakes.

FIGURE 8: Sketch Niagara Falls in your notebook.

waterfall is made. **Niagara Falls** has been made in this way.

Using the Information

1. List the names of the Great Lakes in your notebook.
2. Why is there a border shown in the middle of four of the lakes?
3. What other regions do scientists believe have been shaped by huge sheets of ice?
4. Sketch a map of the Great Lakes Lowland in your notebook. Include the Niagara Escarpment. Name the three lakes which surround it.
5. Sketch and label a scarp in your notebook.

What is the climate like in the Great Lakes region?

The climate in this region is made up of cold winters and hot summers. The winters are so cold that large parts of the lakes freeze. Ice stops ships from sailing on them from December to April. Although the summer temperatures are hot, lake waters warm very slowly and stay cold all summer long.

The Great Lakes region is in the path of many storms which cross the continent.

Because of this, day-to-day weather can be quite different. This is especially true in the winter.

Read the Charts

1. How are the temperatures in the four locations the same? Different?
2. How is the precipitation in the four locations the same? Different?
3. How is the growing season in the four locations the same? Different?
4. Write a generalization about the climate in the Great Lakes Region?

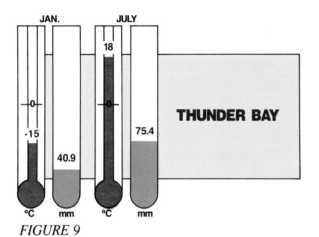

FIGURE 9

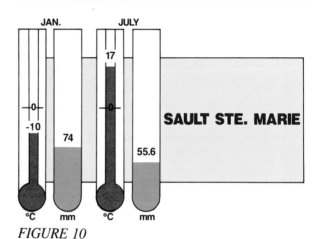

FIGURE 10

Temperature and precipitation charts for Great Lakes centres.

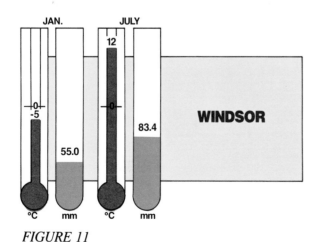

FIGURE 11

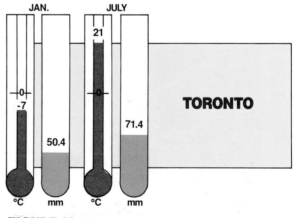

FIGURE 12

What resources are found next to the Great Lakes?

The most important resources found in the region are the lakes themselves. Water from the lakes is used by cities and factories. The lakes provide a perfect waterway for ships. People enjoy the scenery, boating, fishing, and other water sports.

Minerals too are found in the region. Copper, iron ore, silver, lead, zinc, and coal are found in the rock near the lakes. **Quarries** around the lakes provide shale, gravel, and sandstone.

One of the most important minerals found is iron ore. Most of this mineral comes from the northwestern shore of **Lake Michigan,** around Lake Superior and north of **Lake Huron.**

This ore is used to make steel. It is used in plants around the lakes such as the **Stelco Inc.** plant at **Nanticoke.** Nanticoke is located at the mouth of the **Nanticoke Creek** on **Lake Erie.** It is 20 kilometres southeast of **Simcoe,** Ontario.

In choosing a place to build this plant, Stelco Inc. wanted a site
1) close to where the steel would be sold
2) on a body of water
3) close to where iron ore is found
4) close to people so there would be enough workers
5) on rock which would hold up the plant buildings and heavy machinery.

Nanticoke seemed to be the best place for all these things. The company bought 3000 hectares of land for the plant. This included enough land for other industries which Stelco Inc. hoped would become their neighbours.

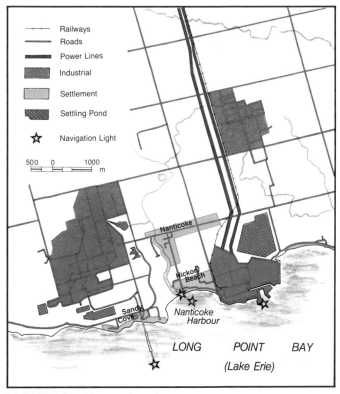

FIGURE 13: Nanticoke, Ontario.

How the steel plant works.

Match each sketch with the correct caption.

- Lake freighters bring coal and iron ore to the pier.
- The coal is put into ovens where it is made into **coke.**
- Coke, limstone, and iron ore are put into a **blast furnace** where they are turned into a kind of iron called **pig iron.**

- The pig iron is mixed with other materials and changed into steel in special furnaces. It is then poured into a **caster** which shapes it into slabs from 25 centimetres x 75 centimetres to 1.84 metres x 22 metres.

FIGURE 14

FIGURE 15

FIGURE 16

FIGURE 17

Cars, stoves, bikes, spoons, skates, and hundreds of other items are made from the steel from plants like the one at Nanticoke.

Before the Nanticoke plant was built, a lot of planning had to be done. There were meetings with people who would live near the plant to explain what was happening. At these meetings the things that the company would do to care for the environment were talked about. The large property was planned so that there would be a lot of green space around the plant. Trees and **berms** were built to block the view and sounds from the plant's neighbours. Berms also block winds off the lake from blowing the piles of coal and iron ore into the air.

How do people earn a living next to the Great Lakes?

The kinds of jobs people have in this region depend very much on the geography. Industries here have grown up because of the ease with which materials can be transported on the Great Lakes. These waterways make it easy to bring iron ore from **Minnesota** and coal from **Pennsylvania** for use in steel mills. Materials from forests, mines, and farms are available. Hydro-electricity is close at hand to run the factories and provide power for the many people who live in the region.

The industries where people find work in Ontario are shown in Figure 18.

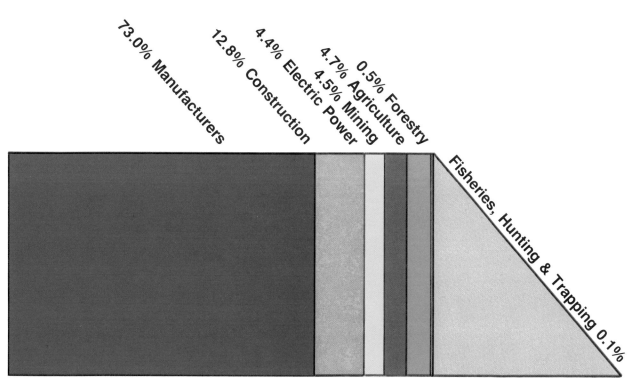

FIGURE 18: Value of industries in Ontario

Using the Information

1. Where are conveyors used in your community?
2. Make a list of ten items your family uses which are made of steel.
3. What things are done in your neighbourhood to block the view of buildings?
4. Draw a sketch map of the Nanticoke plant site in your notebook.

The Van Manen Family

The Van Manen Family are truck farmers. Their farm is located on the **Holland Marsh.** This marshland was drained in the 1920s by settlers from the **Netherlands.** Mrs. Van Manen's grandfather was one of those settlers.

Holland Marsh has fine soil for growing vegetable crops such as carrots, onions, corn, soybeans, celery, beets, peas, beans, and lettuce. The close-by towns and cities are good markets for the food grown.

Farming for the Van Manen family is hard work. They spend many hours cultivating, fertilizing, and caring for their land. The cost of machinery is expensive. Often it is hard to hire people to help them with the work. The Van Manens grow onions, lettuce, and carrots. These crops are boxed, loaded on trucks, and sent to Toronto.

The Van Manens' farm is located on farmland which forms a belt about 600 kilometres long. Land here, especially that close to the **Golden Horseshoe,** is being bought and used for roads, houses, factories, and shopping centres.

FIGURE 19: The Van Manen family.

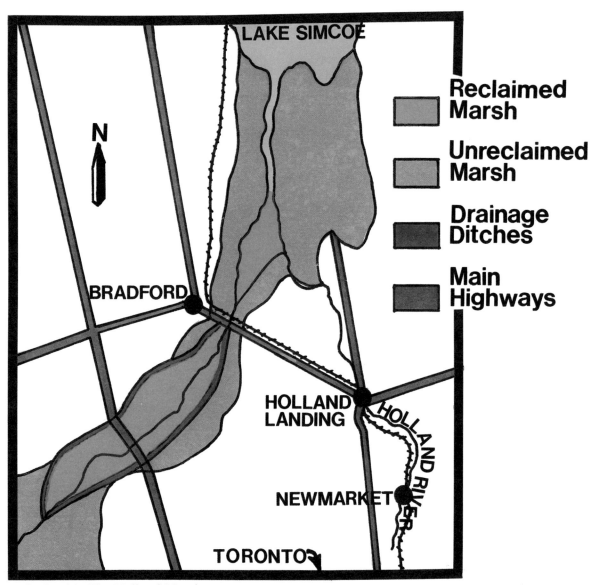

FIGURE 20: The Holland Marsh area.

Read the Map

1. Name the river that drains the Holland Marsh.
2. In which direction does that river flow?
3. Name the lake close to the marsh.
4. Why do you think people from the Netherlands began to farm in this area?
5. List what is needed to grow vegetable crops such as lettuce, celery, and carrots.
6. Why are the Van Manens called "truck" farmers?

The Luzietti Family

The Luzietti family live in a small town on the northern outskirts of Toronto.

Every morning, five days a week, the Luzietti family are up at 6:45 a.m. At 7:30 a.m., Mr. Luzietti is the first to leave for his job working in a large bakery nearby. Fifteen minutes later Mrs. Luzietti leaves with the children. She drives to the nearby elementary school and drops off Gina and Sophia. Tony is dropped off at the junior high school several blocks away.

From there Maria drives on the freeway into Toronto. Most days she arrives at the **publishing house,** where she works, a little after 8:30 a.m. If there is an accident on the freeway or if the weather makes driving dangerous, she may arrive later.

The company Maria works for publishes textbooks for use in schools. Maria is an editor. It is her job to find people to write geography books. She then works with these writers, artists, book designers, and **cartographers** to get books printed and ready for sale to schools.

The decisions Maria makes are important. It costs a lot to publish a textbook. If it does not sell well, the company will not make a profit.

FIGURE 21: The Luzietti family.

Maria makes sure that the books are excellent so that people will want to buy them.

Many of the people Maria works with on the book do not live in Toronto. She often has to spend weekends working with authors who live in other parts of Canada. They come to Toronto to talk to Maria about their ideas. When this happens, Mr. Luzietti and the children often meet her in the city for dinner. They enjoy meeting people from across the country at these dinners.

Using the Information

1. List the industries in Ontario from the most important to the least. Refer to Fig. 18.
2. Although this region is called the Great Lakes, information in the chart is given for Ontario. Why?
3. Which industry do the Van Manen family work in? Maria Luzietti? Mr. Luzietti?

The Konidas Family

The building of the steel mill at Nanticoke, Ontario, by Stelco Inc. was good news for Rose and "Nik" Konidas. Nik works in the construction industry. He is a welder.

Rose and Nik were immigrants from **Greece.** When they came to Canada in 1976, Nik found his first job working on this project. They were able to rent a small house in nearby Simcoe.

Since that time many people have moved to the area. Workers for the steel mill and their families have formed the city of Nanticoke which includes what used to be other towns and villages. Rose and Nik now live in an apartment in this new city.

Life for Rose and Nik has not always been easy. When they first arrived, they did not know how to speak English. They found it

FIGURE 22: The Konidas family.

145

FIGURE 23: Art Yates.

especially hard trying to do all the business that a family must do. Renting a house, buying a second-hand car, and filling out income tax forms was difficult.

Art Yates: Laker Crew Member

Art Yates is a bachelor. His parents live in **Hamilton,** Ontario. Art is a member of the crew on a Great Lakes **freighter** called the **Dominion.** He has kept a diary of a recent trip he took from **Thunder Bay** to Montréal.

Day 1

*This may be my last trip on the **Dominion**, so I thought I would try to keep my diary up-to-date. The Dominion is a **dry bulk carrier.** That means it carries loads like grain which* can be stored loose in the **hold.** It is 200 metres long. There are 33 members of our crew. All night many were busy loading grain. As we moved out onto Lake Superior we passed many other **lakers.***

The weather is good. Water here can be stormy. 10 metre waves are not unusual in such storms.

Day 2

*I slept well last night and came on deck just as we were nearing **Sault Sainte Marie.** (It's called "the Soo"). There is a canal here with a lock to move ships from Lake Superior down to Lake Huron. My sketch shows how this lock works.*

Once through the lock we moved out onto Lake Huron.

Day 3

We spent last night travelling over Lake

FIGURE 24: A Great Lakes dry bulk carrier.

Huron. Our path is toward the south and east. This morning we moved to a busy place at the southern part of the lake. Our ship had to pass from Lake Huron down the St. Clair River, across Lake St. Clair, down the Detroit River, and onto Lake Erie.

We joined many freighters moving along this route. We also met many others taking the same route north. As we floated along we passed cities on both sides of the Detroit River. By afternoon we finally reached Lake Erie. We turned east toward Port Colbourne.

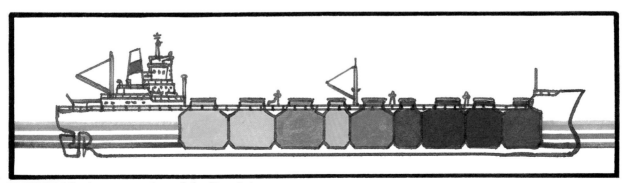

FIGURE 25: A cross-section of the **Dominion.**

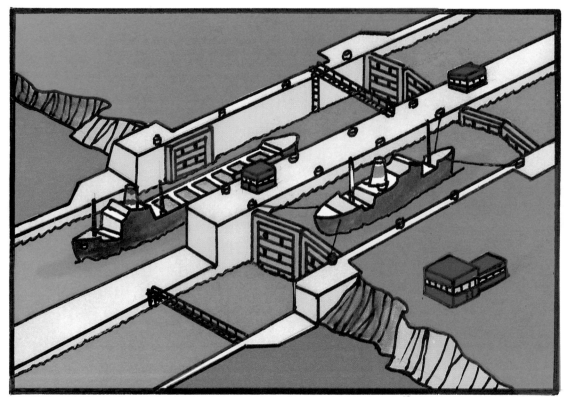

FIGURE 26: *Explain what happens when a ship enters a lock.*

Day 4

At Port Colborne we moved into the **Welland Canal.** Eight locks on the canal take boats down to Lake Ontario. It took us all day to pass through these locks. At dusk we moved onto Lake Ontario. To our **port** side we could see the blinking lights of Toronto.

Day 5

As dawn broke this morning we passed **Kingston** on the north shore and entered the **St. Lawrence River.** We sailed through the **Thousand Islands.** You could see summer cottages on many of the islands. Farther along, we moved into that part of the river which has been made into a canal.

Day 6

It took us all night to go through the seven locks here. After dawn we passed by the city of Montréal. I was taken off the Dominion here so that I could go to the company office to talk about a new job I am interested in. The Dominion will travel 310 kilometres further downstream to **Port Cartier.** There the grain will be unloaded into an elevator. Later it will be loaded onto an ocean freighter and taken to Europe.

Using the Information

1. In which industries listed in Figure 18 do Nik Konidas and Art Yates work?
2. Why would immigrants from other countries, like the Konidas family, move to the Great Lakes region?
3. Make a sketch map showing the route of the Dominion. Label the places Art Yates mentions in his diary.
4. Sketch a cross-section view of a lock in your notebook. Make a list of the things that happen once a ship enters a lock.

FIGURE 27: Part of the urban area around the western end of Lake Ontario.

Where do people live in the Great Lakes region?

This region and the land along the St. Lawrence has more than half of Canada's population. There are more cities with over 100,000 people here than in any other region.

People live in hamlets, villages, towns, and cities across the region. There are strong links between the large cities and the surrounding lands. For example, Toronto is the centre for railways and highways in the Great Lakes region of Canada. They bring the natural resources from the Plains and Canadian Shield regions to the city. Thousands of factory workers, clerks, and managers have jobs because of these links.

The pattern around the western end of Lake Ontario is a collection of **urban** centres. In many places these cities join each other. They are linked as products move from one city to the next. As the products move from place to place they are partly made, finished, and finally sold.

Read the Map

1. List the string of cities on Lake Ontario beginning with **St. Catherines**.
2. Which is the largest city shown?
3. List some problems cities this close together might have.

Wrapped around the western end of Lake Ontario is an area called the "Golden Horseshoe." This horseshoe-shaped area stretches from **Oshawa** to St. Catherines, Ontario. It is about 150 kilometers wide. It is called "golden" because of the great number

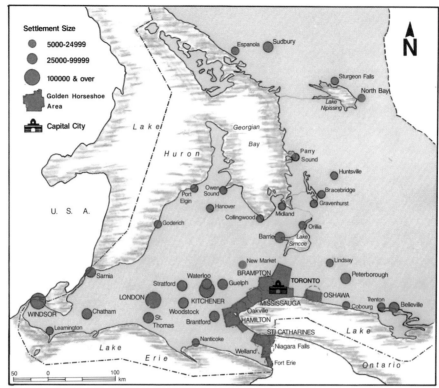

FIGURE 28: Describe the settlement pattern shown on the map.

of factories, businesses, and banks found there, and because the people there are able to earn good wages.

In the middle of the golden horseshoe is the city of Toronto. Toronto is a huge Canadian city.

Antonella Scozza and her family recently moved to Toronto from **Genoa, Italy.** One of the first things they did after arriving was to send the following letter telling about their new city to relatives in Genoa.

FIGURE 29: Antonella and her brother Luciano.

Dear Gina and Alex,
    We have finally had enough time to look around our new city. What is old to people

150

FIGURE 30: The Art Gallery of Ontario, Toronto.

here seems quite new to us. The site was first important as a fur-trading post. It was used by the French.

When the English took over, the land was bought from the Indians for £1700 and gifts. At this time this part of North America was called **Upper Canada**. The British were in charge and fighting with the Americans. A town to be called **York** was planned. This town grew slowly. In 1813 York was partly burnt down by the Americans. It was really only a small village at that time.

The fort at York was rebuilt after the American raid and is still standing. It was once on the edge of Lake Ontario but it is now surrounded by freeways and railways.

After the war York began to grow. When it became a city in 1834 it was named Toronto. Factories and businesses were started. The people, most of them from England, became

wealthy. Being wealthy did not change the people in one way. They believed that, as the Bible told them, Sunday must be a day of rest. They closed their businesses, stopped other activities, and went to church. Soon the city had the nickname of "Toronto the Good."

We have included a map and some pictures of our new city.

Love Antonella

Using the Information

1. Why is Toronto a good place for a settlement?
2. Why would immigrants settle in Toronto?
3. What settlement problems might the hills north of Toronto bay cause?

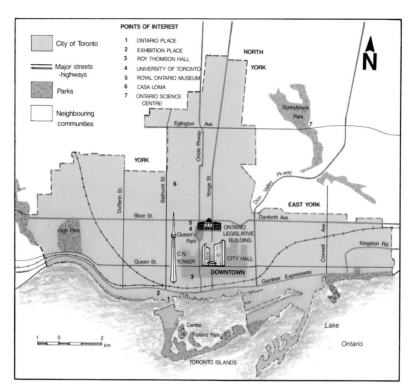

FIGURE 31: Use the map to locate each of the places shown in the following photographs.

FIGURE 32: The CN Tower.

FIGURE 33: Toronto Island.

FIGURE 34: The Ontario Museum.

FIGURE 35: Ontario Place.

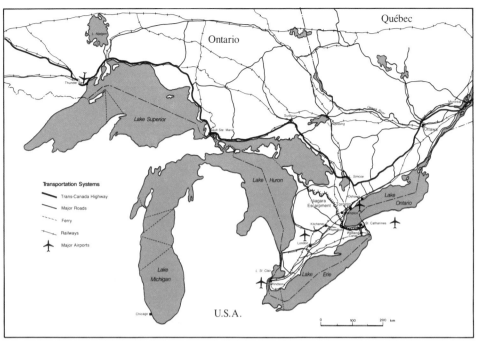

FIGURE 36: Transportation next to the Great Lakes.

How are goods and people transported in the Great Lakes region?

As Figure 36 shows, a transportation **network** has been built. This network moves goods and people between places next to the Great Lakes. The transportation routes have made it easy for cities to spread and new communities to be built.

The network is made-up of different kinds of transportation which are used in the region.

Ships and barges:

This is the least costly way to ship bulky loads. Iron ore, coal, and grain are shipped across the Great Lakes. This is a slow type of transportation and the ships cannot, of course, travel inland in the region. The ice on the Great Lakes interrupts this shipping each year.

Railways:

Next to ships, railways are the least costly way to move loads in the region. They bring in resources from other parts of the country for factories in the golden horseshoe.

FIGURE 37: *Why are so many tracks needed in one place?*

FIGURE 38: *How do trucks and trains "team up" to carry loads?*

Trucks:

Costs of moving loads by truck are more than that of railways. Trucks are used to move goods door-to-door in the region. They are used for short distances and for loads which would not need a full railroad car. They move things faster than trains. Sometimes trucks team up with the railways. Railways may carry truck trailers "piggyback" on long trips.

Airlines:

The airways between Montreal and Toronto and between Toronto and Thunder Bay are some of the busiest in the country. Airline costs are high compared to other ways of moving loads. They are used when products must be shipped quickly and when the products are costly.

FIGURE 39: Not all trains are used to haul goods in the Great Lakes region!

Using the Information

1. Describe the pattern of transportation. What does the pattern look like?
2. Where are the roads and railways closest together? Why?
3. What mode of transportation would you choose to ship:
   • Vegetables from Holland Marsh to Toronto?
   • Cars from Windsor to Thunder Bay?
   • A computer part from Toronto to Thunder Bay?
   • Iron ore from the United States to Hamilton?
   • Coal from the United States to Toronto?

Give a reason for each choice you made.

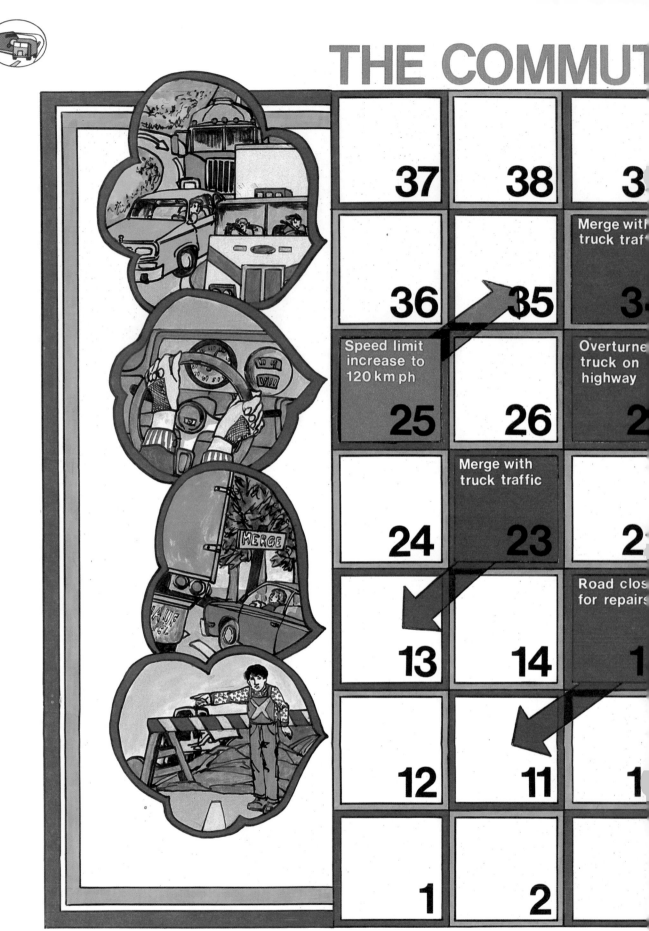

37 | 38 | 3

Merge with
truck traf

36 | 35 | 3

Speed limit
increase to
120 km ph

Overturne
truck on
highway

25 | 26 | 2

Merge with
truck traffic

24 | 23 | 2

Road clos
for repairs

13 | 14 | 1

12 | 11 | 1

1 | 2

FIGURE 40

R GAME

40

41

Home at last!

42

33

32

31

All lights
are green!

28

29

30

21

20

19

16

17

18

9

8

7

w cars on
is stretch

4

5

6

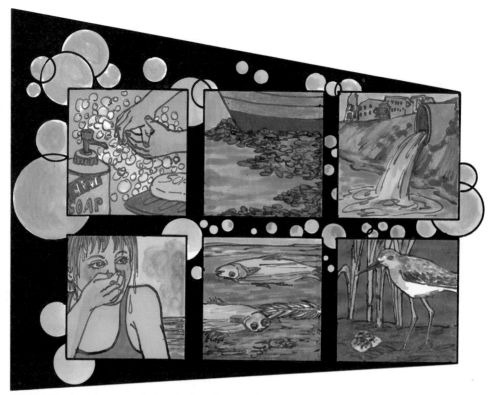

FIGURE 41: Name each kind of pollution shown.

What ideas and inventions have harmed people next to the Great Lakes?

With so many people living and working in the region, pollution has become a problem. One of the biggest problems is that the lakes have become dirty. They have become dirty because sewage and wastes from factories have been dumped into them.

These wastes change the lakes. New soaps have made it possible for us to keep our bodies and clothes clean. However, the chemicals in soapy water help plants called **algae** to grow. Algae can grow so thick that boats cannot move through them. When they die, algae give off a bad smell. This makes it unpleasant along some beaches on the lakes. The dead algae also fall to the bottom of lakes where they rot and take the oxygen out of the

water. When there is no oxygen, the fish living in that part of the lake often die.

Factories around the lake use large amounts of water to make the new products Canadians want. When this water is poured back into the lakes, it often contains chemicals. One chemical called **mercury** can cause people to become ill and even die. Years ago many factories put mercury into the lakes. The fish that have fed in these places cannot be eaten by us.

People living around the lakes caused problems when they used fertilizers and insect killers. These contain chemicals which seeped into the lakes. When birds and fish fed in these areas they became ill, died, or changed. For example, some bird's bodies changed so that their eggs would not hatch.

Acid rain is another pollution problem. Smoke from cars and factories contain a chemical. This chemical floats high into the air. There it mixes with parts of the air and becomes a gas. The sun helps turn this gas into **acids.** These acids become attached to raindrops and snowflakes. This rain and snow then falls and pollutes lakes and rivers. It damages plants and trees. When it falls on buildings it may cause the outside of the building to crumble.

People living next to the Great Lakes are worried about the problem of pollution. They have asked the people they elect to do something about it. Governments in both Canada and the United States are working on the problem. Already, there are laws which do not allow wastes to be dumped into the lakes. It will cost a great deal of money to clean the lakes, but it can be done.

Using the Information

1. In what way have all Canadians helped to pollute the Great Lakes?
2. What might happen to the prices of products, such as cars, if factories have to spend money so that the lakes will not be polluted?
3. List two ways in which those people living next to the Great Lakes can help stop pollution.

Unit 7
What is the land like along the St. Lawrence River?

The St. Lawrence River has always been one of Canada's most important rivers. It was along this river that the first people from Europe travelled. Explorers and fur traders travelled up this stream into the heart of our country. Settlers found the flat land along the river a good place to start farms. In addition the summers were warm, and the soil was good for growing crops.

The section along the river from about **Cornwall,** Ontario, to **Québec City** is a region known as the St. Lawrence Lowland. These lowlands are made up of three plains:

FIGURE 1

FIGURE 2

List the items you see in photographs 1, 2, 3, and 4. Group those items which seem to belong together. Write a sentence about the groups you have made which tells about the St. Lawrence River Region.

FIGURE 3

FIGURE 4

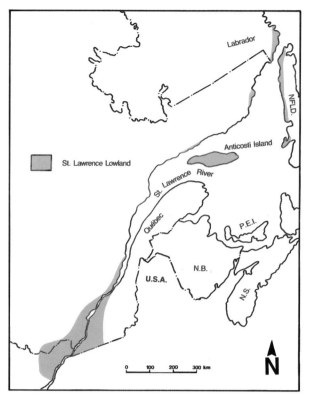

FIGURE 5: Map of the Great Lakes—St. Lawrence Lowland region.

(1) **Quebec Plain**

(2) **Trois Rivières Plain**, and

(3) **Montréal Plain**

Scientists believe that in the past these plains were flooded by the sea for long periods of time. During these floods, layer after layer of **sediment** fell to the sea floor. This sediment is now the rich soil which is so good for growing crops.

The plains are low and flat. In places the plain is only a kilometre or more wide along the river. In these places hills and low mountains next to the plain are part of the landscape. It is easy to farm on the plains but it is also easier to build highways, railways, and cities on flat land. More than six out of every ten Canadians live on the St. Lawrence and Great Lakes Lowlands.

Using the Information

1. Why is the St. Lawrence sometimes called Canada's first highway?

2. Why do farmers prefer to farm on flat land?

3. Most people of the world live on flat land. Can you think of examples of places in Canada which would make this generalization untrue?

162

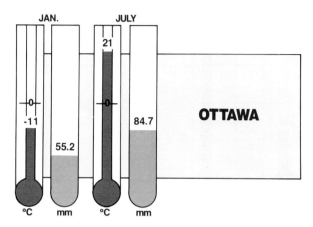

FIGURE 6: Temperature and precipitation chart for Ottawa, Ontario.

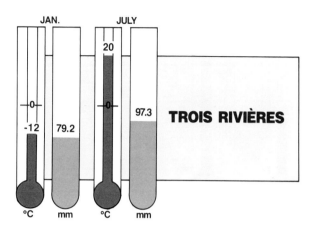

FIGURE 7: Temperature and precipitation chart for Trois Rivières, Québec.

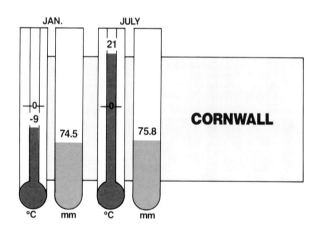

FIGURE 8: Temperature and precipation chart for Cornwall, Ontario.

What is the climate like in the region?

The weather on the St. Lawrence Lowland is hard to describe. In the summer it may be very hot, **humid**, and uncomfortable. In the winter skies may be sunny and clear with temperatures very cold. During the year the climate may change from being like that in the Arctic to that in the **tropics.**

A closer look at three places

In the summer thunderstorms move in from the Canadian Shield. During the winter snowstorms from the Great Lakes may flow as far east as Montreal. Many storms seem to move along the St. Lawrence River valley.

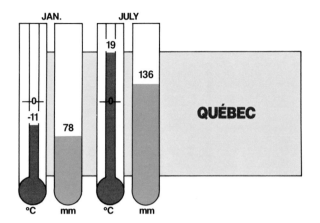

FIGURE 9: *Temperature and precipitation chart for Québec City, Québec.*

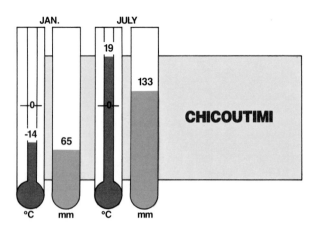

FIGURE 10: *Temperature and precipitation chart for Chicoutimi, Québec.*

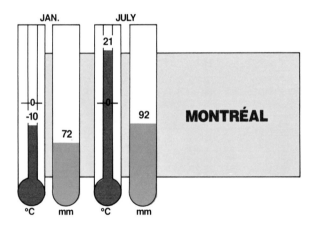

FIGURE 11: *Temperature and precipitation chart for Montréal, Québec.*

Read the Charts

We can gather more information about the climate through using charts like those shown in the above figures.

For example, the highest average monthly temperature in Quebec City is 19.9° C in July. The lowest average monthly temperature is -10° C in January. The yearly **temperature range** is 30.5°.

1. Draw twelve thermometers in your notebook. Use a red pencil to colour in the average temperature for each month in Montréal.

2. Draw twelve **rain gauges**. Use a blue pencil to colour in the average precipitation for each month in Montréal.

3. Which of the three places has the warmest summer? The coldest winter?

4. If you were going to begin a vegetable farm, which centre would you want to be closest to? Why?

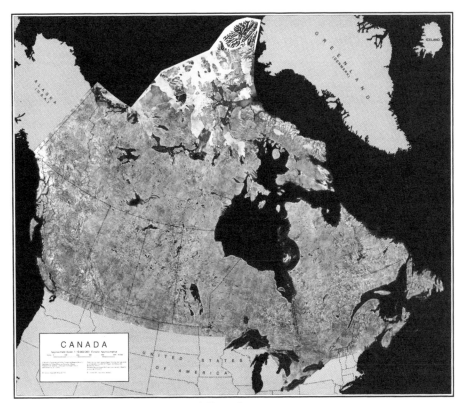

FIGURE 12: A satellite image of Canada.

The range is the difference between the highest and the lowest average monthly temperatures. Can you use the charts shown on page 164 to work out the ranges of temperature for Montréal? Chicoutimi?

In Canada there are about three hundred places where the weather is measured. Some of the measurements taken are used to help scientists called **meteorologists** predict the weather. In recent years meteorologists have been using satellite images to help them do their work.

Use the Image

1. What weather forecast would you give the people along the St. Lawrence River, based on this image?
2. Why is it important for meteorologists to know when a satellite image was taken?
3. List two things about the weather that satellite image gives information about?

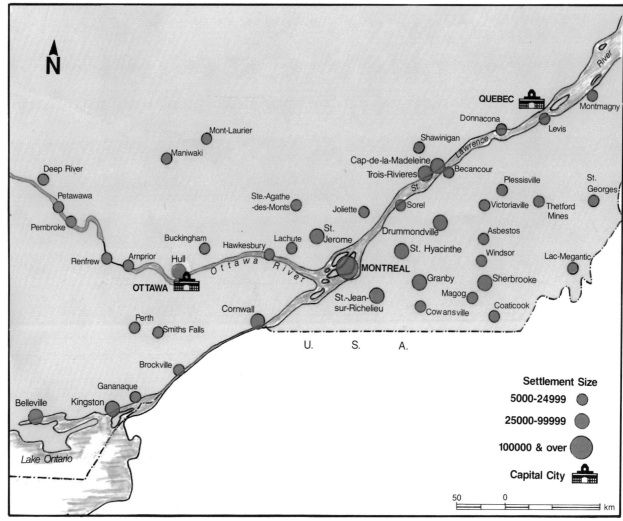

FIGURE 13: Describe the settlement pattern along the St. Lawrence River.

Where do people live?

Some of the cities now found along the St. Lawrence were early Indian settlements. Fur traders and explorers from Europe helped these settlements grow or started new ones. **Cartier** visited the Indian village of **Hochelaga** which is now the city of Montréal. **Champlain** founded Québec City in 1608. It was the centre for all trade and shipping along the river for many years.

The French king gave blocks of land along the St. Lawrence to people called **seigneurs.** Seigneurs were French lords. These lords encouraged settlers from Europe to come and farm on their land. The land of one seigneur is shown in Figure 14.

The block of land was divided into ranges. The first range was along the river. Land was divided into long narrow farms. This let each farm have some property along the river. When farmers died the land was divided among their children. The farms became narrower and narrower.

The seigneur's family lived in a house close to a school, mill, and church. These buildings were often all built by the seigneur.

The land along the St. Lawrence was attractive to settlers. It was flat and easily farmed. The summer temperatures were good for growing crops and the land was easily reached by water from Europe. Canada's past ties to France are still seen in the long narrow farms and settlement patterns.

Today more than half of Canada's population lives in the Great Lakes and St. Lawrence River regions. The area along the St. Lawrence is an area of farms, industries, and many towns and cities.

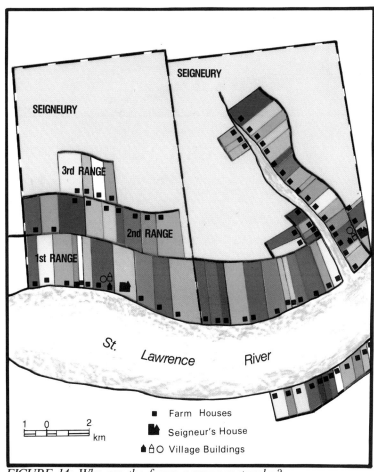

FIGURE 14: Why are the farms narrow rectangles?

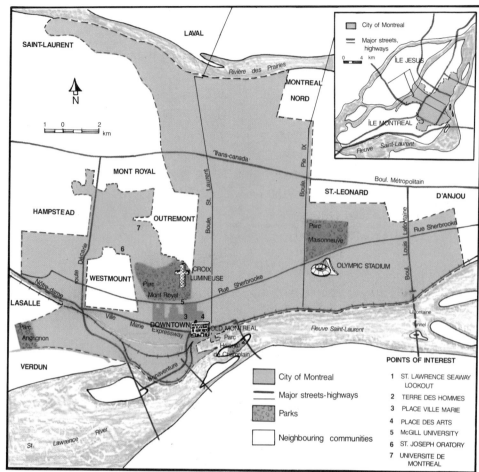

FIGURE 15: Montréal, Québec.

The Largest City: Montréal

When Jaques Cartier visited the Indian village of Hochelaga he was taken to the top of the mountain to see the view. "It is a Royal Mountain" he said. In French *"un mont real."* The name is still with us — Mont Real, which we know as Montréal.

Montréal is the centre of French life in our country. Good French newspapers and books are printed there. French Canadian television plays are produced here. It is the second largest French-speaking city in the world.

Montréal is an important Canadian business, transportation, and trade centre. Many banks and other companies have offices in the city. One of the most important industries found here is oil refining.

A Family moves to Montréal

In 1980 the immigrants who came to live in Canada settled in the provinces shown in Figure 16.

The Luc Family

The Luc family was one of the families counted in the chart in Figure 16. They lived in a country in Asia called **Vietnam** until 1980. They now live in Montréal. Mr. Luc had been an engineer in Vietnam and his wife had been a dressmaker. The Lucs have four children ranging in age from 2 years to 11. In Vietnam, Mr. Luc had become worried about the new government. He wondered if his family would now be safe. He bought tickets on a ship and planned to escape from his country. The family first voyaged to **Hong Kong**. The trip was unpleasant. When the Lucs reached Hong Kong, they were called **refugees.** After many meetings and discussions they were allowed to emigrate to Canada. They had decided to live in Québec. The Lucs spoke French and they knew that other families from Vietnam were living in Montréal. They thought that this would help them learn the ways in Canada more quickly. It is difficult to imagine what it is like to be an immigrant. Here is what the family had to say:

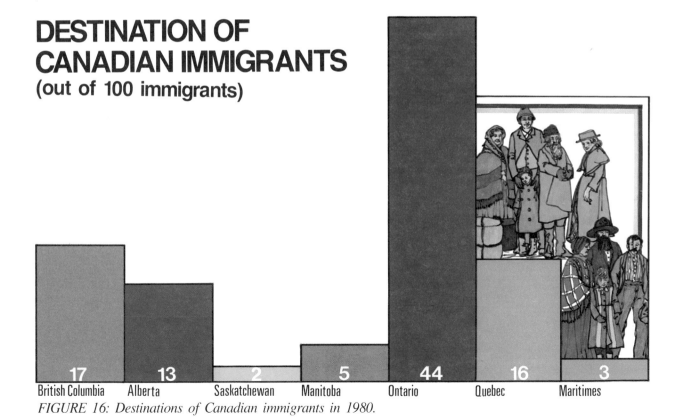

DESTINATION OF CANADIAN IMMIGRANTS
(out of 100 immigrants)

British Columbia	Alberta	Saskatchewan	Manitoba	Ontario	Quebec	Maritimes
17	13	2	5	44	16	3

FIGURE 16: Destinations of Canadian immigrants in 1980.

FIGURE 17: Mr. Luc, Engineer, Age 38
"We landed in Montréal when it was -17°C. I couldn't believe it could be so cold. The first year, especially the winter, I never felt warm once!"

FIGURE 19: Huong, Age 11
"The kids in school were O.K. Some of them were very nice, a few stared and said nothing. One called me a name I didn't understand."

FIGURE 18: Mrs. Luc, Dressmaker, Age 35
"I didn't know what to expect. In school we had talked about Canada, but it always seemed to be wheat fields and farms. I want to learn about Canada but I don't want to forget about our life in Vietnam."

FIGURE 20: Phong, Age 10
"The homes seemed very big and so did the shops and cars. The supermarkets were so huge. There seemed so much to choose from—especially candy!"

FIGURE 21: Yen, Age 8
"Pets! I couldn't understand why people took dogs for walks, called them by name, and fed them special food. It seemed strange to give so much food to an animal. At home many people did not have that much food. I now have a cat, too. I call it Tweetee."

FIGURE 22: Mai, Age 2
"Chà cô." (hello)

Using the Information

1. In which province did most immigrants settle in 1980?
2. In which province did fewest people settle?
3. How do you account for these differences?
4. In which province did the Luc family settle?
5. List five problems newcomers to our country might have.

FIGURE 23

FIGURE 24

Scenes from Montréal.

FIGURE 25

FIGURE 26

Québec City: Our Oldest City

Serge Dumont is a bell-hop in a fashionable Québec City hotel. Serge is very proud of his city and its history. Many tourists visit here. Serge is busiest in February during the world-famous Québec Winter Carnival. At that time tourists come to Québec City to take part in the street dances, observe contests, see hockey tournaments, and view street parades. The winter sports draw many of the tourists. During the Winter Carnival the streets are crowded with visitors admiring the decorations and the ice sculptures which are to be found in the parks and squares.

A highlight of the festival is the canoe race across the ice-choked St. Lawrence River. The Carnival is presided over by the jovial, giant snowman, called **Bonhomme**.

Serge spends much of his day parking cars for the guests of the hotel. The tourists often ask him for directions to Québec City attractions like the **National Assembly**, the **National Battlefields Park** (the Plains of Abraham), **Place Royale**, and the **Hotel-Dieu**. Serge is bilingual and is able to answer the questions of both English and French-speaking guests.

Using the Information

1. Why is it an advantage for people working with tourists to be able to speak more than one language?
2. List some more winter sports which might be added to the Carnival program.

FIGURE 27: Québec City, Québec.

Ottawa: The Capital City of Canada

Although it is not located alongside the St. Lawrence River, **Ottawa** is considered a part of this region. It is located on the **Ottawa River** which flows into the St. Lawrence.

So that we may live together, our country needs laws. Usually every four years we have an election to choose the people who will make those laws. These people make up what we call the Parliament. They meet and discuss the laws we need in the Parliament Buildings in the city of Ottawa.

In countries all over the world the city where lawmakers meet becomes special to the people. They call it their head city or capital city. There, they build buildings for the lawmakers to meet in. Other buildings are built to house collections of items which are important to the country or in which programs may be conducted. Canada's capital city is Ottawa.

Ottawa was picked to be our capital by Queen Victoria in 1857. It was called **Bytown** at that time and quickly had its name changed. By picking Ottawa, the Queen helped stop the arguments among Toronto, Montréal, Québec City, and Kingston: each thought they should be named the capital city.

Stan Gilinski: Guide

FIGURE 29: Stan Gilinski.

Stan Gilinski lives in Ottawa. He is an official guide for the Parliament Buildings. The Parliament Buildings are really three buildings. Mr. Gilinski works in the Centre Block. As he walks to work he approaches the Peace Tower. On the top of the tower a white light is burning. This means the Parliament is meeting. The Peace Tower entrance leads to the House of Commons. The House of Commons is the place where people elected from across the country meet to make and talk about laws.

Mr. Gilinski enjoys his work. He meets the people who make the laws for all Canadians. He also talks to people from all over the country who visit their capital city.

Most of the visitors agree with him that Ottawa is a beautiful city. There are many parks in the city where people can walk and relax. In winter he often goes to the Rideau Canal to skate. Like many people he calls the canal the longest skating rink in Canada. Some streets in the city have been closed to cars and are for pedestrians only. Mr. Gilinski thinks that this is a good idea and he likes to stroll or window shop in this area of the city.

Because Ottawa is the capital of Canada, it is also the temporary home of many people from other countries. People from other countries work with the government of Canada. The places where these people live and work are called **embassies.** At the embassy you will find an **ambassador.** The ambassador from another country often meets with the Prime Minister to discuss problems.

Using the Information

1. Canadian car makers are upset about the number of Japanese cars being sold in Canada. What would you say if you met the Japanese ambassador?
2. An ambassador says that his country is very short of both food and money and wants Canada to help. What would you say to him?
3. An ambassador says that Canada is selling guns to another country which is planning a war. What would you say to the ambassador?

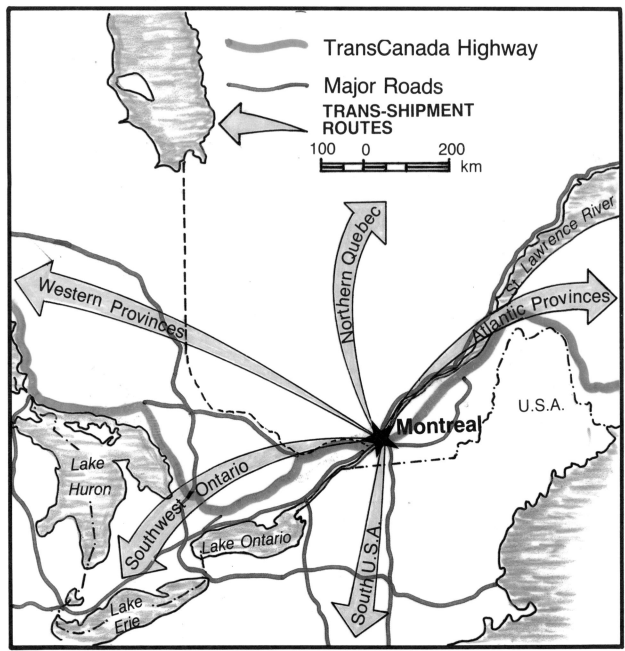

FIGURE 30: Trans-shipment routes from Montréal.

How are people and goods transported along the St. Lawrence River?

In 1535 **Jacques Cartier** reached Hochelaga, a native Indian village, now called Montréal. Shallow water in the river and the **Lachine Rapids** prevented him from continuing his voyage up the St. Lawrence River. In 1825 a canal was built around the Lachine Rapids. This was the first of a number of canals and locks which were built. The goal has been to allow larger and larger ships to sail upstream from Montréal to the Great Lakes.

Montréal became a **trans-shipment** point. Goods were unloaded at Montréal and then transported to other parts of the continent.

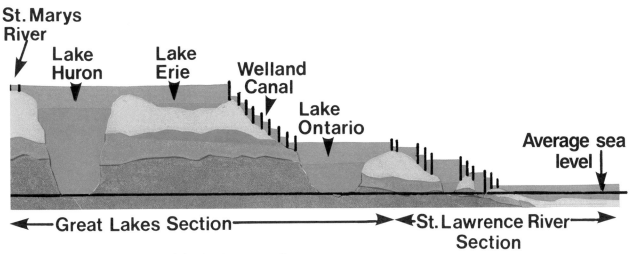

St. Marys River

Lake Huron

Lake Erie

Welland Canal

Lake Ontario

Average sea level

←—Great Lakes Section——————→ ←St. Lawrence River—→ Section

FIGURE 31: Cross-section of the St. Lawrence Seaway.

Goods from the interior were brought overland to Montréal where they were loaded onto ocean-going ships. Montréal gradually grew into a transportation, manufacturing, financial, and cultural centre.

In the 1950s the governments of Canada and the United States agreed to build a seaway so that ocean-going ships could travel up the St. Lawrence River and onto the Great Lakes to deliver and collect cargoes.

Read the Chart

1. Why do you think Canada and the United States wanted to build the St. Lawrence Seaway?
2. Can you explain how a lock works?
3. What is the name of the canal that links Lakes Erie and Ontario?

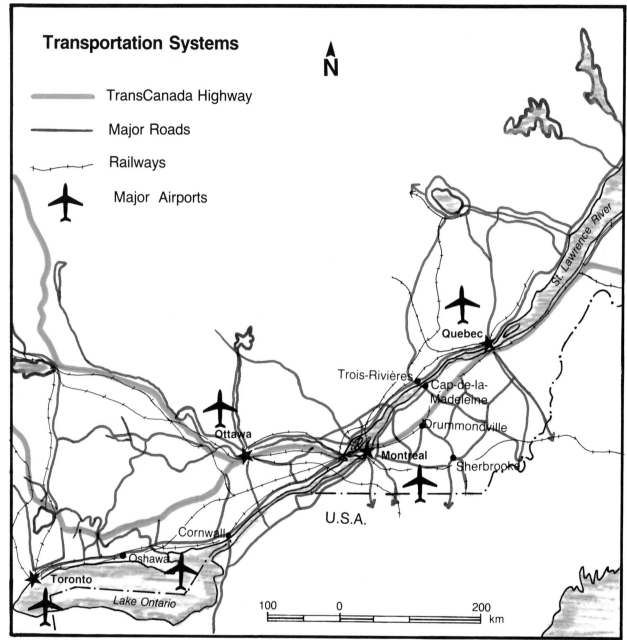

FIGURE 32: *Transportation routes along the St. Lawrence.*

Read the Map

1. What information is shown on the map?
2. Describe where most of the transportation routes are located. Why?
3. Why are railways, waterways, and highways needed in the region?
4. Why might railway companies have not wanted the St. Lawrence Seaway built?

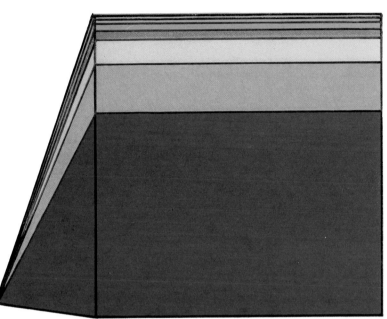

TRAPPING 0%
FISHERIES 0.2%
FORESTRY 1.3%
AGRICULTURE 4.0%
MINING 4.3%
ELECTRIC POWER 7.2%
CONSTRUCTION 16.5%
MANUFACTURERS 66.5%

FIGURE 33: Make a symbol which could be used on the chart for each industry shown.

QUÉBEC INDUSTRIES

FIGURE 34: Helen James.

How do people earn a living?

The St. Lawrence Lowlands are one of the wealthiest regions in Canada. Nearly one out of every six Canadians lives and works here. The value of different kinds of industries for all of Québec is shown in Figure 33. Agriculture, electric power, manufacturing, and construction provide most of the jobs for people in the St. Lawrence River region.

Helen James: Garment Worker

Helen James is an immigrant. She now lives in Montréal where she works in the garment industry. The part of the plant where she works makes T-shirts. Garment factories are part of

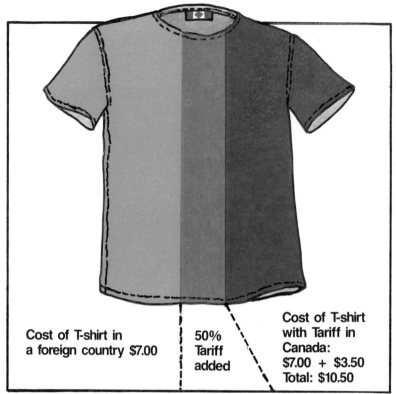

Cost of T-shirt in
a foreign country $7.00

50%
Tariff
added

Cost of T-shirt
with Tariff in
Canada:
$7.00 + $3.50
Total: $10.50

FIGURE 35: Tariffs and T-Shirts.

the manufacturing industries.

The T-shirts are made of cotton. Buyers from all across Canada come to Montréal to see and buy the T-shirts that Helen and her co-workers make. Helen is paid according to the number of T-shirts that she makes. This is called **piecework**. When the women who make the T-shirts have coffee, they often discuss their fear that the factory may have to close. The owner of the plant complains that his workers cannot make T-shirts at a low enough cost. He says that factories outside the country often take away his business because they sell their shirts for less money.

The owner would like to see the government do something about the problem. His solution is to have a **tariff** put on all T-shirts sold in Canada by foreign companies. Figure 35 shows how a tariff would make foreign-made shirts cost more.

Helen has to catch the Metro to work each day. She lives in the suburbs of Montreal. Although Montreal is known for its fine downtown stores, Helen does most of her shopping in a shopping centre near her home.

Helen has a dream. One day she would like to have her own ladies clothing store in this shopping centre. Should Helen locate her store there? If you were giving her advice, where would you tell her to locate the store? Should it be downtown or in her shopping centre? Before answering you might want to consider:

— What type of stores and services are found in small shopping centres?

— Where are most special shops such as those which sell only one kind of thing located? Why?

— What do shoppers think about when they choose a store in which to shop?

FIGURE 36

FIGURE 37

FIGURE 38

FIGURE 39

FIGURE 40

FIGURE 41

FIGURE 42

FIGURE 43

Using the Information

1. Some workers are paid for each hour they work. Others, like Helen, are paid for each article they make. Which do you think is the best way to be paid? Why?

2. Many immigrants work in jobs like the one Helen has. Can you suggest reasons why?

3. Why can factories in other countries make T-shirts which cost less than those made in Canada?

4. Should tariffs be put on things that are sold in Canada? Give one reason for having tariffs. Give one reason for not having tariffs.

FIGURE 44: Reg Harris.

Reg Harris: Garbage Collector

Reg Harris is a garbage collector. The work he does is important if we are to keep our communities clean and healthy. Each day Mr. Harris follows a route to collect garbage. The material he collects is taken to a dump. The dump they are using now is called a landfill. Garbage will be dumped, packed down, and covered with layers of earth. One day a park will be built on the top of all the garbage.

Choosing a place for landfill can be difficult. Some of the items considered include:

What is the land like?

Will the underground water be safe?

Is the ground likely to move or slide?

Is it easy to get to by road?

Is it close to electricity?

Is it far away from the water supply?

Who owns the land?

Are there laws which tell how the land must be used?

Do people in the community close to the dump want it to be located there?

Does the government want the dump?

Is it close to where the garbage will be collected?

Is there a large enough piece of land for a dump?

How will the land be used in the future?

Mr. Harris often wonders why we throw away as much as we do. He really thinks that more use could be made of what some people call garbage. Some things he knows could be used again or re-cycled.

Which of the items in Figure 46 could be re-cycled?

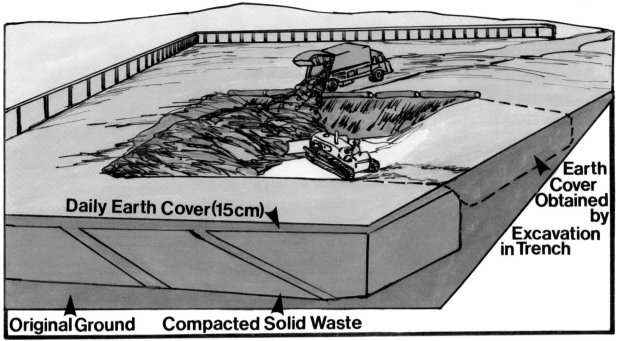

FIGURE 45: *Where our garbage goes.*

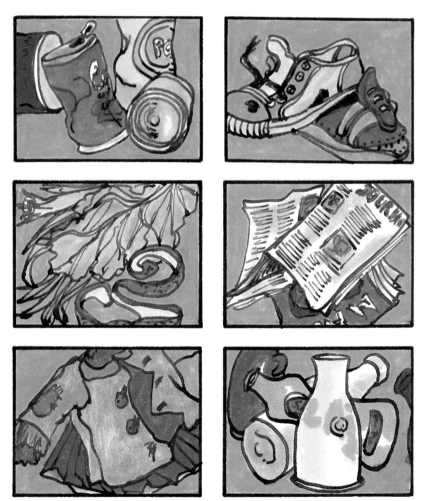

FIGURE 46: *Which of these items could be re-cycled?*

183

A Problem to Ponder

What to do with dangerous chemicals?

Carol and Steve Moody live several kilometres away from a dump. There are signs telling people to keep out. However, Carol and Steve have seen a wheel in the dump that they feel would fit the wagon they use to deliver newspapers. Mr. and Mrs. Moody have warned the children that they must not enter the dump because of the dangerous chemicals found there.

I am sure it is alright to go into the dump just to get that wheel. We don't need to touch anything else.

I am not so sure. Some chemicals can be dangerous even if you don't touch them! How will we know if we are near them.

Surely they wouldn't keep really dangerous chemicals in a city dump where little children could touch them.

You never can tell. People do not always follow the law when they put things in dumps.

Leon Franks: Firefighter

Leon Franks is a firefighter. He has been carefully trained and has learned that firefighters do not spend all their time putting out fires. Much of Mr. Franks' time is spent checking equipment, but he and his partners are ready to help at the ring of an alarm.

Distress calls go to a control centre. The duty officer there decides which fire truck can

FIGURE 48: An emergency.

get to the emergency fastest. When their station is signalled they can be ready to leave in two minutes. This includes the time it takes to put on their special clothing and equipment. The siren on their truck warns traffic to move aside so that they get help to people who need it as quickly as possible.

A racing fire truck may be going to several different kinds of emergencies. What could a firefighter do to help in each of the following situations?

FIGURE 47: Leon Franks.

FIGURE 49: A house is flooded by a rising river.

FIGURE 50: A truck driver is trapped in the cab after an accident.

Some emergencies firefighters face.

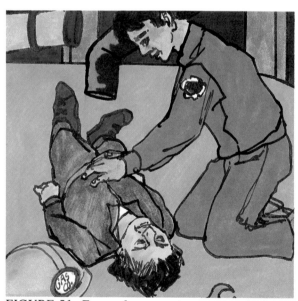

FIGURE 51: Fumes from a poisonous gas leak overcome a man.

FIGURE 52: A child with her head stuck in a fence.

FIGURE 53: The Mahé family.

The Mahé Family: Farmers

If you live in a town or city you probably go to the supermarket fairly often. There, aisle after aisle of food awaits your choice. Some of the food can be stored in your home for a long time before being used. Some of the food is called perishable and it has to be used fairly quickly or else kept in a refrigerator. Farms are often found close to cities so that the farmer has a close market for the products he raises. The Mahé family live in what are known as the **Eastern Townships** of Québec along the St. Lawrence River. These townships are east of Montréal. Unlike the square or rectangle farms of the plains, many farms in Québec are long, narrow strips. The farms were planned this way. It allowed each farmer to have land along the river for water and transportation and farmhouses which would be closer together.

The Mahé farm is a mixed farm. Most of the cash money comes from the sale of fresh milk to dairies in Montréal. A part of the farm is used to grow vegetables which are sold

during the summer to a nearby cannery.

Monique and Louis Mahé are hoping to retire in the next few years and to have their daughter Hélène and her family take over the farm. Monsieur Mahé and Madame Mahé are beginning to find looking after milk cows every morning and evening hard work. They have a modern milking barn which helps speed up their work but, like most dairy farmers, they have few days off.

The Mahé family depends upon many other people in order to make a living from their farm. They must have help harvesting hay each year. Often they must buy what they need from other farmers. Dairy trucks pick up the milk from their farm and a number of different people are needed to repair the special kinds of farm equipment that they use.

Using the Information

1. How are the jobs Helen James, Reg Harris, and Leon Franks work at the same? Different?
2. List ways in which these workers depend upon each other.
3. How is the Mahé farm different from farms on the plains? The same?

FIGURE 54: Countryside near the Mahés' farm.

Unit 8

What is Atlantic Canada?

Atlantic Canada is the name given to the provinces of Newfoundland and Labrador, **Prince Edward Island, Nova Scotia, New Brunswick,** and the part of Québec which borders the mouth of the **Gulf of St. Lawrence**.

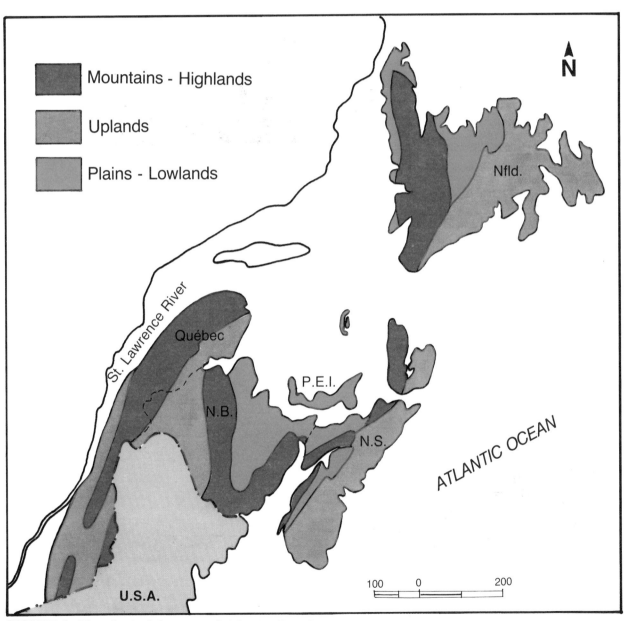

FIGURE 1: The physical features of Atlantic Canada.

FIGURE 2

FIGURE 3

List the things you see in figures 2, 3, 4, & 5. Group those things which seem to belong together. Write a sentence based on each of these groups. Which sentences tell you something about the Atlantic region?

FIGURE 4

FIGURE 5

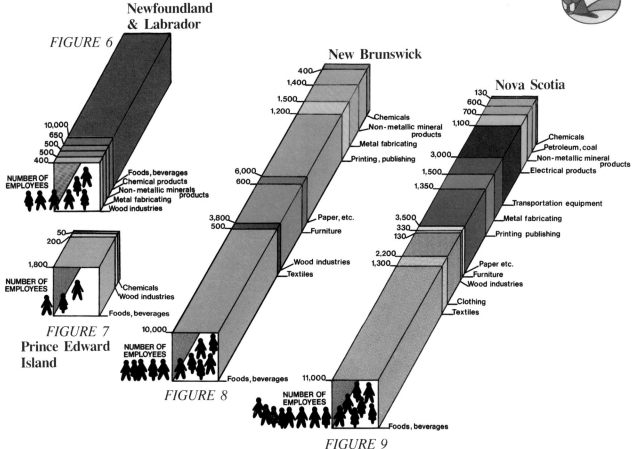

Newfoundland & Labrador

FIGURE 6

NUMBER OF EMPLOYEES

- 10,000
- 650
- 500
- 500
- 400

Foods, beverages
Chemical products
Non-metallic minerals products
Metal fabricating
Wood industries

FIGURE 7
Prince Edward Island

NUMBER OF EMPLOYEES

- 50
- 200
- 1,800

Chemicals
Wood industries
Foods, beverages

New Brunswick

- 400
- 1,400
- 1,500
- 1,200

Chemicals
Non-metallic mineral products
Metal fabricating
Printing, publishing

- 6,000
- 600

Paper, etc.

- 3,800
- 500

Furniture

Wood industries
Textiles

- 10,000

NUMBER OF EMPLOYEES

Foods, beverages

FIGURE 8

Nova Scotia

- 130
- 600
- 700
- 1,100

Chemicals
Petroleum, coal
Non-metallic mineral products
Electrical products

- 3,000
- 1,500
- 1,350

Transportation equipment
Metal fabricating
Printing publishing

- 3,500
- 330
- 130
- 2,200
- 1,300

Paper etc.
Furniture
Wood industries
Clothing
Textiles

- 11,000

NUMBER OF EMPLOYEES

Foods, beverages

FIGURE 9

Most important industries in the Atlantic region provinces.

What resources are found in Atlantic Canada?

Read the Graphs

To read these graphs you will have to understand what the term *manufactures* means. The graphs above will help.

1. What do the graphs describe?
2. Figure 6 shows some things that are manufactured. Think up at least five other items that are manufactured. Sketch symbols which could be used to show them in a graph like the one shown in Figure 6.
3. Name the industry which brings in the most money in each province.
4. Why is the most important industry not the same in each province?

5. Which items in the graphs are not resources but depend on resources?
6. Which part of the Atlantic region is not shown in the graphs?
7. How might the graphs change over a number of years for a province?

Much of the region is fairly rugged and covered with forest. Figure 1 shows how different the region is from province to province.

The rock found under the region contains such metals as iron ore, lead, gold, and copper. In some places large amounts of coal are to be found. Some of these coal deposits stretch out under the ocean. North America's oldest industry, fishing, is carried out in the region. It was fish that first attracted Europeans to North America.

What is the climate like in the Atlantic Region?

Weather is very important to the lives of many people in the Atlantic region. People who work in the fishery watch the weather closely. Storms, heavy fog and even icebergs are things they must constantly be on the watch for. Weather in the region can change quite suddenly.

Temperatures and rainfall can be quite different as you move from place to place in the region. The ocean has much to do with the climate of the region. It helps to make the temperatures milder.

Ocean currents help shape the climate of the Atlantic region. When a warm current of water meets a cold current, the result is usually fog, rainfall or snowfall. Northern areas of the region tend to have shorter summers and colder winters than southern areas.

Read the Charts

1. How do these temperatures compare to those in your community?
2. Why is the winter temperature for **Fredericton** colder than for the other places shown?
3. The following are the **frost free days** in three of the places shown below.
   Halifax May 13 - Oct. 12
   St. John's June 1 - Oct. 10
   Charlottetown May 8 - Oct. 19
   How many frost free days are there in each community?

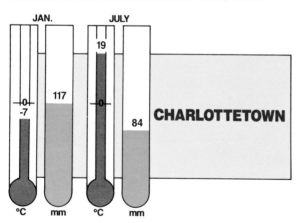

FIGURE 10

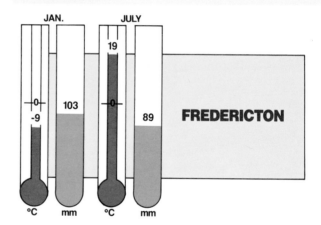

FIGURE 11

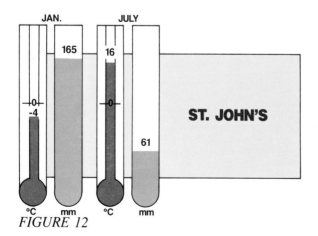

FIGURE 12

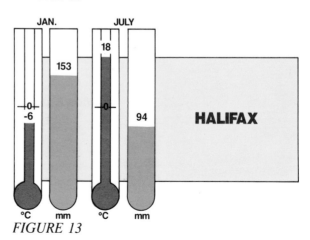

FIGURE 13

How do people earn a living?

Many of the people who live in Atlantic Canada live close to the ocean. The ocean has always been very important to people who live in this region. For hundreds of years, fishing fleets from Europe came and fished in the waters in this area. Many early settlements were started by these fishermen. The Atlantic region was fought for by the French and the English for many years.

Henri Bouchard: Student

Henri Bouchard is a student who attends college on **Cape Breton Island.** During the summer, Henri is a guide at **Louisbourg.** To become a guide, Henri had to learn about the history of Louisbourg.

Louisbourg was a great French fort that protected the entrance to the **St. Lawrence River.** Louisbourg guarded the river and served as a shelter and supply base for fishermen who came to fish the **Grand Banks.**

This fort was considered to be so strong that the British would never capture it. As Henri takes tourists around the fort, he points out that the walls were nine metres high. There was a twenty-four metre-wide ditch around the fort. Large guns pointed out over the harbour and land.

Tourists are interested to learn that over five thousand people lived in the fort. It contained a large hospital, some barracks, a convent and school, enormous warehouses, and fine homes. Lumber, bricks, flour, and fish were sent to France in exchange for wine and other goods.

FIGURE 14: Henri Bouchard.

FIGURE 15: Cannons helped defend Louisbourg.

Attacking the fort was very difficult. The guns had to be unloaded from ships; roads had to be made through the rocks and swamps before the British could reach the hills overlooking the town. While this was happening, the French guns fired from the fort on the attackers.

The year was 1744, and before they finally took the fort, the British had to lay **siege** for forty-nine days.

A year later the British and French signed a peace treaty. Fort Louisbourg was given back to France. But, it wasn't long before the two countries were back at war. And, by then, the French had made Louisbourg stronger than ever.

The fort was attacked by the British for the last time in 1758. One of the English soldiers who fought in that battle was James Wolfe. His guns did a great deal of damage. Once again the French had to surrender the fort.

The British decided the fort had to be destroyed. In 1760, sailors and soldiers

worked for months blowing up the fortress. Louisbourg was left in ruin.

Today, Louisbourg is a national park. Money is being spent to try to rebuild the fort. Guides such as Henri provide us with an idea of how the first European settlers in the Atlantic region lived.

Using the Information

1. Find the name of a community near where you live where the population is 5000 people.
2. Why are forts not built today?
3. Why did the British destroy Louisbourg?
4. Find out how people in forts protected themselves from sieges.
5. Why did both the French and the English want this region?

FIGURE 16: Louisbourg was a huge fort.

FIGURE 17: Mr. & Mrs. Hurst.

The Hursts: Farmers and Hosts

Mr. and Mrs. Hurst live on Prince Edward Island. They are farmers but add to their income by providing **"bed and breakfast"** to tourists during the summer season.

The Hursts grow potatoes on their farm. The rich red soil is good for this purpose.

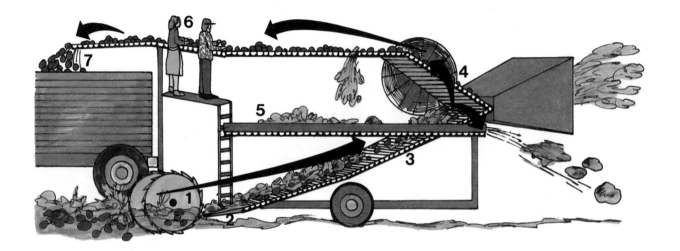

FIGURE 18
1. Two steel plates dig up roots of potatoes.
2. Pointed steel plates scoop up everything.
3. Weeds, stones and potatoes move on to the conveyor.
4. A large fan blows away some of the debris.
5. Stones and other heavy objects fall.
6. Pickers sort out the potatoes.
7. Potatoes drop into a truck.

Prince Edward Island has been called 'a vegetable garden fenced by sandy beaches and protected by the sea.'

The Hursts have seen many changes in their lifetimes. They remember when being a potato farmer was back-breaking work. The potatoes had to be planted and picked by hand. The weeds that grew had to be hoed by hand. Today there is machinery which plants and harvests the crop.

Using the Information

1. Make a list of workers whom you depend upon so that you might eat french fries at a restaurant.
2. What kinds of transportation are needed to move potatoes from farms to homes?
3. What might happen if the workers at the supermarket went on strike?

FIGURE 19: *Tourists stay with the Hursts during the summer months.*

Every year thousands of visitors from other parts of Canada and the United States visit Prince Edward Island. They come to enjoy the fine beaches or to attend summer festivals.

Many of these tourists like to meet the people on the island. One way they can do this is to stay at homes such as the Hursts' which offer 'bed and breakfast'. Here they may get to know the people better, and they usually pay less money than it would cost to stay in a hotel or motel.

For many years Mr. and Mrs. Hurst have opened their home to such guests. They enjoy talking with visitors from all over the continent.

FIGURE 20: *How to make french fries! Think of captions for these illustrations.*

Using the Information

1. Name the two industries which the Hursts are part of.
2. What resources do the Hursts use?
3. What other services do tourists coming to Prince Edward Island need?
4. How are the Hursts linked to other parts of Canada?

FIGURE 21: An off-shore drilling platform and a supply ship.

Mary Somners: Geologist

When people think of Atlantic Canada the product that often comes to mind is fish. However, that may soon change. Newfoundlanders are now caught up by a boom in gas and oil exploration.

Mary Somners is a **geologist**. She works for an oil company that is spending large amounts of money exploring the rock under the ocean for oil. It is her job to look at the samples of rock which are drilled from the ocean floor. The kind of rock found helps tell whether or not oil will be discovered.

Drilling for oil offshore is very costly. Large drilling platforms are anchored to the ocean floor with huge chains. The drilling platform looks like a floating island.

Working on such rigs may be dangerous. Storms on the **Grand Banks** cause huge waves. Icebergs would cause great damage if they floated into a rig. Drilling often stops when the winter gales arrive. In one storm, the drilling rig called **Ocean Ranger** was sunk. All the workers lost their lives.

The crews who work on the platform are flown there by helicopter. There about 65 people working on the rig at one time. After working for a number of weeks on this sea drilling rig they are flown back to Newfoundland for a rest.

Using the Information

1. What is Mary Somner's job?
3. Why don't workers live all year round on the rig?
4. How might oil be transported from the rig to the mainland?

FIGURE 22: Mary Somners.

FIGURE 23: John Connors.

John Connors: Ferry Worker

John Connors lives in the Newfoundland community of **Argentia.** During the summer, John works on a car ferry which brings both goods and tourists to the island.

The Connors family have lived here for many years. John enjoys the foods which are special to Newfoundland. "Jiggs Dinner" is one of his favourites. It is a stew which contains beef, pork, potatoes, carrots, turnips, cabbages, and salt. It is served with side dishes of pease pudding (mashed split peas) and duffed pudding (raisins and molasses in a suet pudding).

A few years ago John looked forward to working at an oil refinery which had been built at **Come By Chance**. The refinery was built but it has since been closed. John hopes that one day it will open.

200

FIGURE 24: An Atlantic pilot whale.

John's grandfather used to talk about the whaling industry which had employed people at **Chapel Arm.** Schools of **Atlantic pilot whales** were driven into shallow waters and killed. Their meat and oil was sold. Now this industry is gone. Since 1973, it has been unlawful to kill pilot whales.

Many things seem to have changed in this region. It has caused problems for some workers. They now talk about "goin' down the road." This means moving somewhere else to find a job.

John does not like to think that one day he, too, might have to move away. There may be jobs in other parts of Canada, but it means leaving behind family, friends, and a way of life that he loves.

Using the Information

1. Locate Argentia, Come By Chance, and Chapel Arm on a map of Newfoundland.
2. People often move from place to place in Canada to find jobs. Where might John and his neighbours go to find work.
3. What happens to workers when a factory or business closes?

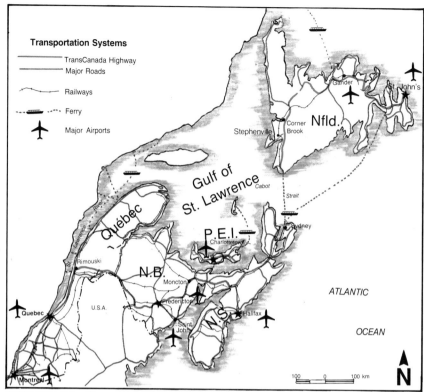

FIGURE 25: *Transportation in the Atlantic region.*

How are goods and people transported in the region?

Read the Map

1. What kinds of transportation are shown on the map?
2. Between which communities could you travel by ferry?
3. Which is the longest ferry trip shown?
4. List the communities you would visit as you travelled from St. John's to **Stephenville** by rail.
5. What do the routes the highways and railways follow tell you about the land?

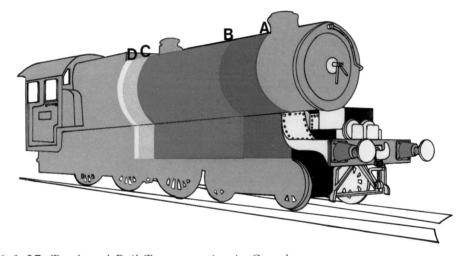

FIGURES 26 & 27: *Truck and Rail Transportation in Canada.*
A. *Fabricated materials*
B. *Crude materials*
C. *Food, feed, beverages and tobacco*
D. *End products*
E. *Live animals*
F. *General cargo*

In Canada, great distances and a small population have caused problems. Often customers live far away from places where the goods they want are made. Many times natural resources are located long distances away from the plants which will make them into products. Figures 26 & 27 show some of the kinds of freight moved across the country and how much of it is moved by truck and rail.

A large variety of goods are transported within and outside of the Atlantic region. How these loads are carried is very important. Figure 28 shows how much freight is carried by rail and truck in four regions in Canada.

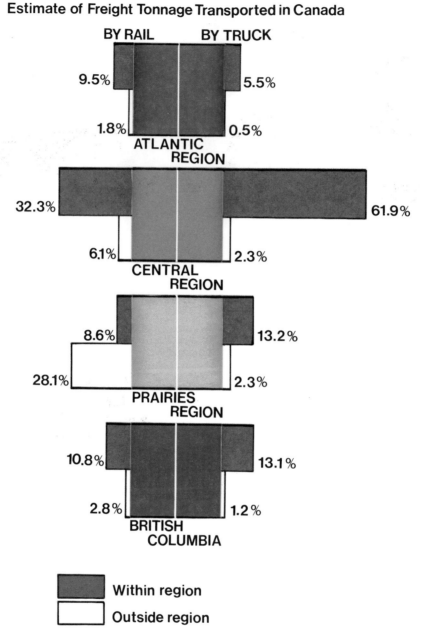

FIGURE 28: *Estimate of freight transported in four regions.*

Reading the Graphs

1. What information is shown in each graph?
2. What is the largest amount of freight carried by truck? By rail? Can you give reasons for this difference?
3. Why does the graph on page 203 show no live animals carried by rail?
4. What is the most important way of moving freight in the Atlantic region?
5. Why is water transportation not used on the prairies?
6. Which region carries the least freight by truck? The most?
7. Write a sentence that describes transportation in the Atlantic region.

FIGURE 29: David Billings.

David Billings: Trucker

David Billings is a long-distance truck driver. His next trip is from **Blacks Harbour**, New Brunswick, to Montréal. Blacks Harbour has some of the largest canneries in Canada.

David's truck carries canned sardines and herring to Montreal. On the return trip he will be loaded with manufactured goods. These goods will be sold in stores. David plans his trips carefully. Once he reaches **Fredericton** he will travel on the **Trans-Canada Highway** to Montréal. The distance to Montréal from Blacks Harbour is 1030

FIGURE 30: Sardines in Blacks Harbour.

kilometres. David hopes he will be able to average about 80 kilometres an hour. If he leaves at 4 a.m. what time will he arrive?

Truck drivers face a number of problems. Choose a partner and see how long it takes you to travel from Blacks Harbour to Montréal.

As David drives to Montréal he will pass a number of road signs. Look at the signs shown in Figure 31. Do you know what each means?

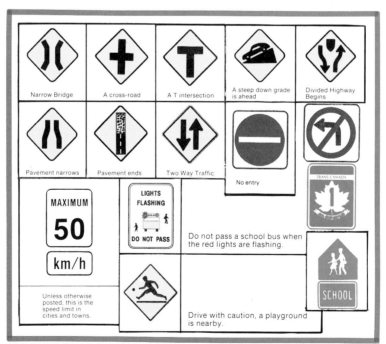

FIGURE 31: Why are symbols used instead of words for many road signs?

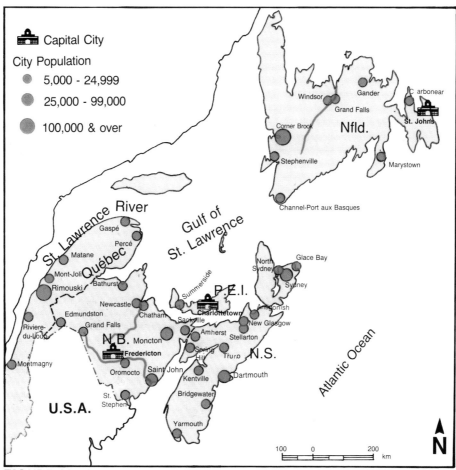

FIGURE 33: *Central places in the Atlantic region.*

Where do people live?

When the explorer **John Cabot** sailed along the shores of what we now call the Atlantic region, he was very impressed by the number of fish found there. Soon many fishermen came to the region.

The names given to places along the shoreline tell about the luck which some of these fishermen had. **Gripe Point, Famish Cove, Bleak Island,** and **Empty Basket** all remind us of what these people experienced hundreds of years ago on their voyages.

Although we study the Atlantic region as a whole, parts of it were settled quite differently.

Read the Map

1. Make a list of the largest settlements in the region.
2. Where are most of the largest settlements located? Why?
3. Where are most of the settlements located? Why?

207

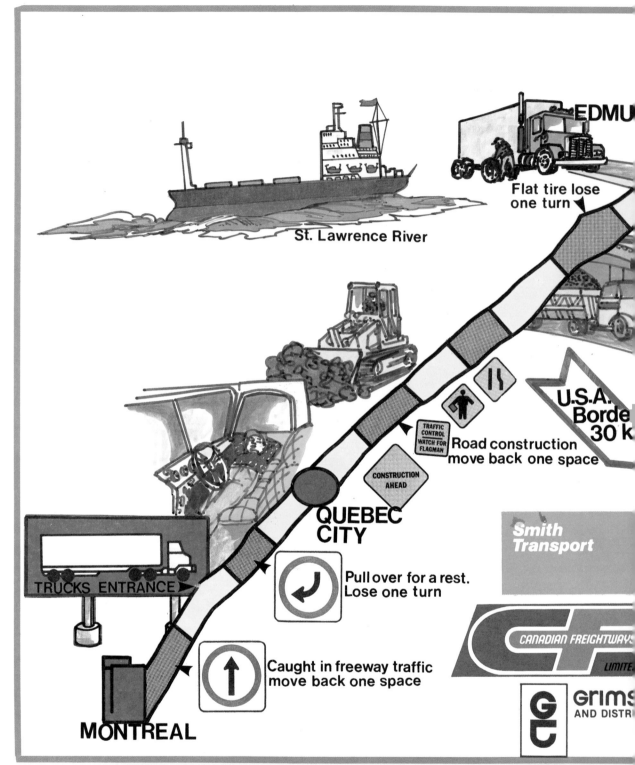

St. Lawrence River

EDMU

Flat tire lose one turn

U.S.A. Borde 30 k

TRAFFIC CONTROL WATCH FOR FLAGMAN

Road construction move back one space

CONSTRUCTION AHEAD

Smith Transport

QUEBEC CITY

Pull over for a rest. Lose one turn

CANADIAN FREIGHTWAYS LIMITE

TRUCKS ENTRANCE

Caught in freeway traffic move back one space

GD Grims AND DISTR

MONTREAL

FIGURE 32

Montréal and back

Play this game with a classmate. You will need a marker and a die. You each have to try to get your truck load to Montréal and back as quickly as possible. The first one to make the round trip is the winner.

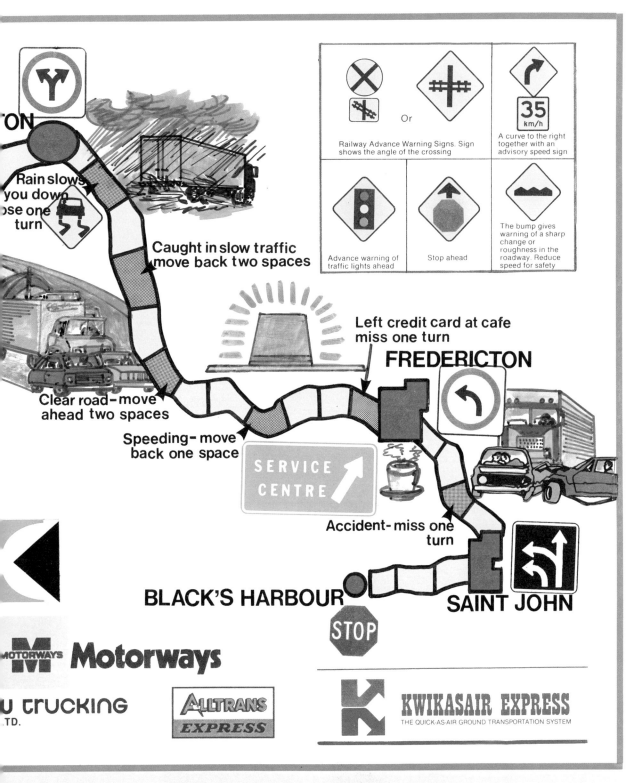

Railway Advance Warning Signs. Sign shows the angle of the crossing

Or

A curve to the right together with an advisory speed sign

35 km/h

Advance warning of traffic lights ahead

Stop ahead

The bump gives warning of a sharp change or roughness in the roadway. Reduce speed for safety

Rain slows you down lose one turn

Caught in slow traffic move back two spaces

Clear road – move ahead two spaces

Speeding – move back one space

Left credit card at cafe miss one turn

FREDERICTON

SERVICE CENTRE

Accident – miss one turn

BLACK'S HARBOUR

STOP

SAINT JOHN

Motorways

U TRUCKING LTD.

ALLTRANS EXPRESS

KWIKASAIR EXPRESS
THE QUICK-AS-AIR GROUND TRANSPORTATION SYSTEM

Rules:

1. You must shake an even number to show your truck is loaded.
2. Each of you must shake the die in turn and move the number of spaces you have rolled.
3. If you land on a red space, obey the instructions.
4. You must roll an odd number once you reach Montréal before you may begin the return trip.

Newfoundland

It is believed that Viking explorers visited Newfoundland around the year **1000.** It was **John Cabot** who named the island after he found it on a voyage in **1497.**

After it was claimed by England in **1583,** there was a dispute over whether a settlement should be allowed or not. Merchants in England did not want settlers on the island. They argued that such settlements would grow quickly and compete with them for the fish. Laws were passed that made settlement almost impossible.

It was England's battles with France that ended this ban on settlement. First, when they were busy fighting the French, the English found it hard to stop settlers from moving to the area. Second, since the English fishing boats might be destroyed, it seemed better to have fishing settlements which could supply fish.

Nova Scotia, Prince Edward Island, and New Brunswick.

The first Europeans who came to this part of the region left many descriptions of what they saw. **Jacques Cartier**, a Frenchman, wrote about Prince Edward Island: *"All this land is low and the most beautiful it is possible to see, and full of beautiful trees and meadows."*

Indian tribes lived in these provinces when people from Europe first arrived. The French gave the name **Acadia** to the area we now know as Nova Scotia and New Brunswick.

A French settlement was begun at **Port Royal.** It was one of three early settlements which are shown in Figure 34.

Early settlers from France farmed the

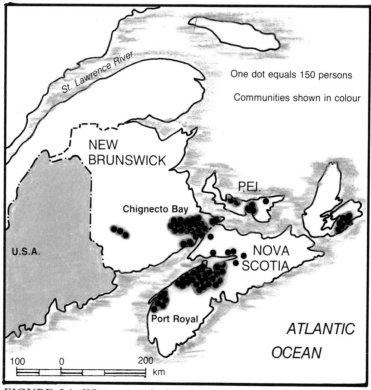

FIGURE 34: Where people lived in the Maritimes in 1748.

low marshlands. Crops such as cabbages, apples, corn, wheat, rye, oats, and peas were grown. Some farm animals were also raised.

Read the Map

1. What information is shown on the map?
2. What was the approximate population of the region in 1748?
3. Where are the settlements located? Why?

The English soon became interested in Acadia. In **1749, Halifax** was started as a naval port. One of the saddest events in Canadian history happened in **1755**. It was that year that the English expelled the French settlers.

In **1776** the **Loyalists** from the United States began to arrive. These were people who remained loyal to England and did not want to stay in the United States if it was not a part of Britain.

In New Brunswick the fish trade brought the first settlers. They found the soil rich and a plentiful supply of timber. Soon the forests were being used not only for buildings and fuel but for shipbuilding. Timber was taken to England for shipbuilders there. It was also used by shipbuilders in New Brunswick.

The timber trade brought more people who settled in the valley of the **St. John River** and along the eastern coast.

Settlement in Prince Edward Island came later. Acadian-French settlers farmed the land along the river valleys and coast. In **1766** it was divided into sixty-seven lots. These lots were sold in London. However the buyers were not attracted to the property they now owned. It was not until **1875** that the property was bought by the government and sold to farmers in the area. This was the beginning of the growth of settlement.

	A	B	C
Nova Scotia			
New Brunswick			
Prince Edward Island			
Newfoundland			

Using the Information

1. Make a timeline for the years 1000 to 1800. Place the events you have read about on the timeline.
2. Complete the chart above in your notebook, based on your timeline.

What ideas and inventions might help people in the Atlantic region?

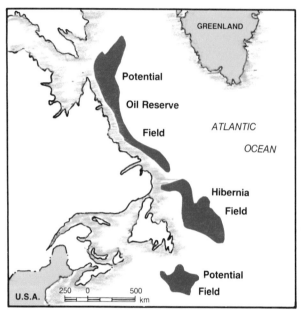

FIGURE 35: *What problems must be solved to get oil from an undersea oilfield?*

Building oil rigs for use in the ocean is very difficult. Huge waves, ice, and icebergs may destroy them.

The rigs are anchored to the ocean floor by chains and may be moved out of the path of a threatening iceberg.

Dr. Jarlan, a Canadian scientist, has a different idea for these rigs. He has planned a rig, called the **Ninian**, which is now used in the **North Sea**.

The Ninian, shown in Figure 36, is built using one of Dr. Jarlan's inventions. It is called the **Jarlan perforated wall.** This special double wall is used in harbours around the world to help control the waves which would pound onto shore. It is made of double concrete walls. The ocean side wall has rows of round holes just over one meter in diameter. The space between the walls fills with water when waves hit. Figure 37 shows how these concrete walls work. When

FIGURE 36: *The Ninian platform.*

FIGURE 37: Jarlan perforated wall.

a wave hits the wall the water flows into the holes in the wall. Then, the water flows back out of the wall and helps to stop the next wave. The wall absorbs the energy of the waves.

Off shore oil rigs like the Ninian use this invention. They have Jarlan walls around the base to stop ocean currents and at the surface to stop wave action.

These rigs built of concrete will last for fifty years or more. They will not rust in the water the way steel rigs do. They do not need painting every few years.

Using the Information

1. What does *perforated* mean?
2. How is a Jarlan wall different from ordinary sea walls?
3. What advantages does a Jarlan rig have over an ordinary sea platform?

Conclusion

FROM SEA TO SEA

We have now had a look at our country from sea to sea. As we moved from region to region we found ways in which Canadians' lives are the same and ways in which they are different. Our explorations have taken us from the Pacific Ocean to the Atlantic Ocean. We have looked at fellow Canadians from our southern border with the United States to our northern polar limits. Now that we have studied our country region by region, let us go back and take a look at Canada as a whole.

What is the land we live on like?

1. Look back through the text. List the pages on which photographs and illustrations of Canadian landscapes may be found. As you review these images, think of how the land across the country varies. Write a generalization which tells about the landscape of Canada.

2. Review the temperature and precipitation charts shown for each region in the text. List the pages on which these charts are found. Based on this information, what might you write about the weather to someone who was thinking about moving to our country?

3. Canada is a land of many resources. Review each region and compile a list of the resources found in our country. Draw a symbol beside each item on your list to show how these resources might be shown on a map of Canada.

4. Many Canadians have a special feeling about their country. They share those feelings through art, music, stories, and poetry. Charles Sangster, Pauline Johnson, Katherine Hale, and Sir Charles G.D. Roberts are just a few of the Canadians who have written poems about our land. Try to find a poem which has been written about the region in which you live.

Who are the people of Canada?

5. Review the sketches of Canadians shown in the text. Write the name and occupation of each person or family you have identified. Next, write a generalization about the people of Canada based on these illustrations.

6. Immigrants bring with them many ways of living from their homelands. Make a list of the Canadian families you have studied which would help prove this statement.

How are Canadians linked together?

7. Look back at the illustrations of transportation, communication and inventions in each of the regions. Make a list of the pages on which you find these photographs and drawings. Place a star next to each illustration which shows a connection between Canadian regions.

8. The flow of goods in Canada could be compared to the flow of blood through your body. Using this comparison write a paragraph explaining where the heart of transportation in Canada is located. Write several more paragraphs explaining where the major arteries are located.

Where do Canadians live, meet, and do business?

9. Review the illustrations of central places in the text region by region. Use the information to complete the chart below:

Central Place	Name	Page No.
Hamlets		
Towns		
Small Cities		
Large Cities		
Metropolitan Areas		

10. Look back at the maps in the text which show where central places are located. Then, write a generalization about the location of central places in Canada.

What problems do Canadians face?

11. Throughout our history, Canadians have had to solve problems. Some are solved quickly and others take many years to resolve. Review each region and list one problem people in that region must face. List what you think the solution to the problem should be.

We have learned about our country through the use of maps, case studies, photographs, drawings, and writings. As you grow older you will learn more about Canada. You will have the opportunity to visit or live in different parts of our country, watch television, read and continue your school studies.

Trying to understand your country will be a lifelong task. Hopefully, the big ideas represented by symbols in this book will help you make sense of the information you gather. These symbols should also be useful to you as you try to understand what happens in parts of our country away from your own.

Topical Index

A

acid rain, 159
An Issue to Ponder
Should northern rivers be dammed to make electricity?, 112
A Problem to Ponder?
A National Park on Ellesmere Island: Do We Need One?, 103-104
What to do with dangerous chemicals?, 188
apparent path of the sun, 80
Atlantic Canada
defined, 189-190
resources, 191, 212-213
landscape, 190-191
climate, 192
occupations, 193-201
transportation, 202-208
central places, 209-211
avalanches, 44

B

bush pilots, 132

C

Canadian Shield
defined, 105
how formed, 107
landscape, 105-107
climate, 108-109
resources, 110-118
central places, 119-122
central places
defined, 4
cordillera region, 36-39

plains region, 55-62
northern, 90-98
Canadian Shield, 119-122
Great Lakes region, 149-152
St. Lawrence River region 166-175
chemist, 71, 72-73
climate
of Canada, 11
cordillera region, 24-25
plains, 52-54
north, 80-83
Canadian Shield, 108-109
Great Lakes region, 138
St. Lawrence River region, 163-165
Atlantic region, 192
cordillera region
defined, 21-23
climate, 24-25
resources, 26-35
central places, 36-43
transportation, 44-47

D

Dempster Highway Game, 100-101
driller, 71, 73
drought, 53

E

electricity, 34

F

farms
changes, 56-57, 61-63
corporation, 61-63
grain, 61
irrigated, 67 - 70
truck, 142-143
mixed farm, 187
potato, 195-198
ferry worker, 200-201

Photograph Credits

Reidmore Books gratefully acknowledges the assistance and cooperation of the following individuals, corporations, agencies, and governments in providing photographs used in this book. Entries are by page number, coded as follows:
U—upper; L—lower, left; R—right.

Glossary

A

acid [ASS id]
A sour liquid that can eat away things.
acid rain [ASS id RANE]
Rain mixed with acid which destroys things on which it falls.
algae [AL jee]
A group of water plants.
ambassador [am BASS a door]
An important person sent by the government to another country.
apparent path [a PARE unt PATH]
The path the sun seems to take across the sky each day.
Atlantic pilot whales [at LAN tik PIE lut WALEZ]
A kind of whale.
axis [AK sis]
An imaginary, straight line on which the earth turns and that runs through the earth from the North Pole to the South Pole.

B

backhoes [back HOEZ]
Machines for digging ditches.
balsam fir [BALL sum FUR]
An evergreen tree of North America.
barren [BARE en]
Not growing anything.
berms [BURMZ]
Small hills.
binders [BIND urz]
Machines that cut grain and tie it in bundles.
blast furnace [BLAST FURN is]
a furnace that turns minerals into liquid by blowing air into the bottom of the furnace to make a great heat.
boundary [BOWN dree]
A line or border between things such as countries.
buoys [BOYZ]
Objects which are anchored in the water to help warn or guide boats.

C

capital city [CAP u tul SIT ee]
The city where the government meets.
cartographers [car TOG ru furs]
Makers of maps or charts.
caster [KAS tur]
A small wheel.
charter airline [CHAR tur AIR line]
An airline which rents airplanes to others.
chemistry [KEM is tree]
The study of what things are made of.
chinooks [shuh NOOKS]
Warm winter winds that blow across Alberta and Saskatchewan.
chums [CHUMZ]
A kind of Pacific salmon.
claim [KLAME]
A piece of public land that a person marks out for their own.
claim stakes [KLAME STAKEZ]
Pointed sticks which miners drive into the ground to mark the boundary of their property.
coho [KOE hoe]
A kind of Pacific salmon.
coke [KOKE]
A fuel made from soft coal.
conifers [KON u furs]
A large group of evergreen trees and shrubs most of which have cones.
cordillera [kor DILL air uh]
A chain of mountains.
corporations [kor puh RAE shuns]
Groups of people who join together to run a business or other enterprises.

D

decayed [di KAY duh]
Became rotten.
delta [DEL tuh]
The earth and sand dropped by a river which builds up into a three sided shape at the river mouth.
depth sounder [DEPTH SOWN dur]
A machine used on ships to measure how deep the water is.
diesel generator [DEE zell JEN ur ay tur]
A machine that runs on diesel fuel and makes electricity.

221

drill bits [DRILL BITZ]
Tools which are turned to make holes.

droughts [DROUTZ]
A long time without rain.

dry bulk carrier hold [DRIE BULK KARE ee ur HOLD]
Storage space underneath the deck of a ship used to store grain and other dry cargoes.

E

earth satellites [URTH SAT uh LITES]
Objects which revolve around the earth.

elevators [ELL eh vae turz]
Buildings for storing grain.

embassies [EM beh sees]
The offices and home of an ambassador in a foreign country.

escarpments [ess KARP munts]
Steep slopes or cliffs.

exports [eks PORTS]
Articles sent out of a country.

F

federal government [FED ur ul GOV urn ment]
The government of a country such as Canada.

fibres [FIE burz]
Parts that look like threads.

fjords [FEEORDZ]
Long narrow bays between mountains or cliffs.

freighter [FRATE ur]
A ship or airplane for carrying goods.

G

generalization [JEN ur uhl uh ZAE shun]
A rule based on many facts.

geology [JEE all uh jee]
The subject that studies the earth's crust.

geologist [JEE all uh jist]
A person trained to study the earth's crust.

government [GOV urn ment]
A way of ruling.

grain terminal [GRANE TUR muh nell]
The storage buildings for grain at the end of a railway.

H

hemisphere [HEM uh sfeer]
Half of a globe.

hopper cars [HOP ur KARZ]
Railway cars in which materials such as coal are hauled for dumping someplace else.

humid [HUE mid]
Damp or moist.

hydro-electricity [HIE droe i lek TRISS uh tee]
Electricity made by using water power.

I

Inuit [in OO it]
Name preferred by the people who were once called Eskimos.

Inuk [in OOK]
One Inuit person.

Inuktitut [in OOK ti toot]
The language spoken by the Inuit.

J

Jarlan perforated wall
[JAR lan PER fuh rat ed WALL]
A wall built with holes in it to control water. Named after the inventor.

L

lakers [LAKE urz]
Ships which travel on the Great Lakes.
latitude [LAT i tood]
East west lines on a map or globe that measure the distances from the equator.
laws [LAWS]
Rules which help people live together.
lichens [LIE kenz]
Small plants, like moss, which often grow on rocks or trees.
local government [LOW kel GUV run ment]
People elected to run the government in a town, village, city, etc.
longitude [LON jeh tood]
North-south lines on a map or globe that measure distances from the line numbered zero which passes through Greenwich, England.

M

marshland [MARSH land]
Low land covered at times by water.
mayor [MAY ur]
The person elected to head the government of a town, city, etc.
merchant vessels [MER chunt VESS uls]
Ships used to transport goods.
mercury [MUR kure ee]
A silver-white liquid metal.
mercy flights [MER see FLITES]
Airplane trips to help people in trouble.
meteoroligists [mee tee ur ALL uh gists]
People who study the weather and atmosphere.
metropolitan area
[met ruh POL uh tun AIR ee uh]
A place which contains a large city and the surrounding communities.
minute [mi NOOT]
Very small.
mobile homes [MOE bile HOMEZ]
Homes which may be easily moved.
moraines [muh RANEZ]
The piles of rocks, sand, and other materials left behind by glaciers.
muskeg [MUSS keg]
An area of wet ground covered by decaying plants such as moss.

N

network [NET werk]
A combination of things which make a pattern.

O

observatory [ub ZUR vu toe ree]
A place with equipment for looking at the stars.
ore [OR]
Rock, sand and soil which contains a metal.

P

permafrost [PER mu frost]
Ground that is always frozen.
physics [FIZ iks]
The subject that deals with the actions of energy or matter such as light, sound, and electricity.
pig iron [PIG IRUN]
Iron as it first comes out of the blast furnace.
pinks [PINKS]
The smallest kind of Pacific salmon.
ports [PORTZ]
Harbours or places where ships can load and unload.
portages [POR tijz]
Carrying boats over land from one body of water to another.
prairie [PRARE ee]
A large area of rolling grassland with few trees.
prefabricated [pre FAB ru kate ed]
Parts made beforehand for putting together later.
premier [PRE mure]
In Canada, the head of the government of a province.
prime minister [PRIME MIN iss tur]
In Canada, the head of the government of the country.
province [PROV ens]
In Canada, one of the parts into which the country is divided.
publishing house [PUB lish ing HOWS]
A company that is in the business of preparing books, newspapers, or magazines for sale.

pulpwood [PULP wood]
Wood which is mashed for making paper.

Q

quarries [KWORE eez]
A place where stone is dug or blasted out.

R

rain gauges [RANE GAGEZ]
Containers which measure the amount of precipitation which falls over a period of time.
refugees [REF u jeez]
People who escape from one country and go to another to be safer or more secure.
regions [REE junz]
Places or parts of the earth's surface.
reservoirs [REZ ur vwarz]
Places where water is collected and stored.

S

sediment [SED uh ment]
Material which settles to the bottom of a liquid.
seigneurs [SEEN yerz]
In French Canada a people who were granted land.
self-propelled harvesters
[SELF pruh PELL ed HAR vist ers]
Crop cutting machines which contain their own engine.
service jobs [SURV iss JOBZ]
Jobs where people do things which help other people.
siege [SEEJ]
Surrounding a place in order to capture it.
snowmobiles [SNOWE muh beels]
Vehicles used for travelling over snow and ice.
snowsheds [SNOWE shedz]
Long sheds built over railways or roads to protect them from snow.

sockeyes [SOCK ize]
A kind of salmon.
spruce [SPRUSE]
An evergreen tree with needle shaped leaves.
stooked [STUKED]
Bundles of grain arranged together so they will stand up and dry.
stopes [STOPES]
Tunnels in mines where ore is taken from.
summer fallow [SUM ur fal O]
Farm land which is left unseeded for a season.
summit [SUM it]
The top.

T

tariff [TAR if]
A tax which must be paid on some imports and exports.
temperature range [TEM per uh chur RANGE]
The number of degrees between two temperatures.
territory [TAIR uh to ree]
An area or region of land.
threshed [THRESHED]
Separate seeds from other parts of the plant.
trans-shipment [TRANS SHIP ment]
Ship across land or water.
tree line [TREE LINE]
A line across northern Canada beyond which trees do not grow.
tuktuk [TUKTUK]
An Inuit name for caribou.
tundra [TUN druh]
A large treeless area in the arctic.

U

urban [UR bun]
Having to do with towns and cities.
utilidor [u TILL i door]
An above ground passageway containing heat, water, and sewer pipes to homes in some northern communities.